Then

THE END

The Jewish Unveiling of Revelation and The End

By Al Garza Th.D, PhD

Published by The Jewish Institute.com

TABLE OF CONTENT

The Secret Rapture?..pg.7

    Early Years..pg.9

    The Word Rapture...pg.10

    Then The End...pg.15

    The Jewish O.T...pg.18

    The Jewish N.T...pg.21

The Mystery of the Resurrection.........................pg.25

    Jesus Died...pg26

    Jesus Has Risen..pg.28

Errors in Eschatology....................................pg.31

    Daniel 9...pg.31

The Mark of the Beast....................................pg.52

    The Discovery..pg.52

    No Antichrist?...pg.55

The Olivet Discourse.....................................pg.62

    The Fig Tree...pg.74

    This or That Generation?.................................pg.75

The Book of Revelation...................................pg.77

    Date of Composition......................................pg.78

    The Temple in Rev.11.....................................pg.79

    The Seven Kings in Rev.17................................pg.82

    The Jews in Revelation...................................pg.84

    Conclusion...pg.86

    The Theme of Revelation..................................pg.87

    Audience Relevance.......................................pg.88

Contemporary Expectation......................pg.89

Theme Statement................................pg.90

Thematic Character..............................pg.94

Thematic Flow....................................pg.100

The Divorce Decree Against Israel.............pg.102

The Execution of the Judgments...............pg.105

Conclusion.......................................pg.106

The Millennium..pg.109

The One Thousand...................................pg.110

The Early Church................................pg.112

Be Ready...pg.118

Bibliography..pg.120

INTRODUCTION

America has gone prophecy mad. If you read popular magazines like Time or Newsweek or if you read the technical scientific journals and Christian books of our day, you will find prophetic studies on what the world will be like in the 21st century and beyond. The secularists do not call these projections concerning the future "prophecy," for that word has too much of a religious connotation. Instead of "prophecy" they use the word SCENARIO, which means to outline the coming events. I am sure that you have been required to read much in the area of secular and Christian scenarios. Some of you have read 1984, The Biological Time Bomb, or any number of the multitude of books which seek to tell us what the future holds. Among such other books is the Left Behind series which are mainly fiction in story format. The Christian in the 20th century can take advantage of the present popularity of prophetic studies in the secular and Christian world by putting forth intelligibly the divine, inspired scenario of coming events, While the world can only guess about the future the Christian has a sure word of prophecy (II Pet. 1:19). We know through Scripture the main points of the future. We must, therefore, be prepared-to give a logical and reasonable reply to anyone who questions us concerning the prophetic hope within our hearts. This will be in obedience to I Pet. 3:15:16. If you have read in a prophecy book that Jesus will probably return before the year 2012 is over, would you apply to graduate school? Not if you believed the book. Time is too short. The gains would be too far away in time. Question: *Should you*

For over 160 years, pastors, and authors have been telling Bible-believing Christians that Jesus is coming soon to "rapture" His Church to heaven. This means that nothing a person can do to build a legacy on earth will survive the 3.5-year Great Tribulation period that will begin 3.5 years after the "secret" Rapture. They have been paralyzed by Rapture Fever. ***Rapture Fever*** is a study of the paralyzing effects of a doctrine that was invented in 1830. It is time to reclaim the future for the Church of Jesus Christ, and in doing so, reclaim the present. It is time to seek the cure for Rapture Fever.

All over the world today there is an awakening to the near return of the Lord Jesus Christ, and a growing interest in the signs of the times. As Bible believing Christians we rejoice at this phenomenon, yet sad to say, in almost every case the doctrine of the Lord's return has been mixed in with the teaching that He will return first secretly and 'rapture' or take away His Church. Although Church History will show that such a theory has only come into prominence over the last one hundred and fifty years, today it is spreading like wildfire, in books, and even films, and accounts for the teaching in 90% of Full Gospel and Fundamentalist Churches and Bible Colleges, world-wide. This being the case it is our duty as students of God's prophetic Word to examine this doctrine of the Secret Rapture, and ask ourselves, "Is it Scriptural?" We must not divide the church over how Jesus will return but unit together that he will return.

THE SECRET RAPTURE?

When we remember that the Secret Rapture theory was virtually unheard of and untaught until around 1830, it is essential to examine its origins first. Such a teaching was unknown to the early Church Fathers e.g. Justin Martyr, Irenaeus, and Tertullian, who were convinced that the Christian Church would pass through great tribulation at the hands of the antichrist system before the return of the Lord. Furthermore the Rapture theory was not taught by the great stalwarts of the Reformed Faith - Huss, Wycliffe, Luther, Calvin, Knox and Cranmer or even by the Wesley brothers in the 18th Century. Whence this teaching therefore and where came did this novel idea arise?

At the time of the Reformation, the first Protestants widely believed and taught that the Papacy was antichrist, and the Roman Church the Harlot System of Revelation 17. It therefore became necessary for certain Romish theologians to take the pressure off the Pope by inventing a new school of prophetic interpretation now known as Futurism. It was a Jesuit priest named Ribera (1537-1591) who first taught that the events prophesied in the books of Daniel and Revelation would not be fulfilled until three and a half years at the end of the age when an individual world dictator called Anti-Christ would arise. Thus Ribera laid the foundation of a system of prophetic interpretation of which the Secret Rapture has now become an integral part.

Nevertheless in spite of the efforts of false prophets like Ribera and Cardinal Bellarmine it was not for another two and a half centuries that the Jesuit fables began to gain acceptance by Evangelical Christians. In the early 19th Century Futurism entered the bloodstream of Protestant prophetic teaching by three main roads:

(a) A Chilean Jesuit priest, Emmanuel Lacunza wrote a book entitled *'The Coming of Messiah in Glory and Majesty'*, and in its pages taught the novel notion that Christ returns not once, but twice, and at the 'first stage' of His return He *'raptures'* His Church so they can escape the reign of the *'future antichrist'*. In order to avoid any taint of Romanism, Lacunza published his book under the assumed name of Rabbi Ben Ezra, a supposedly converted Jew. Lacunza's book found its way to the library of the Archbishop of Canterbury, and there in 1826 Dr Maitland, the Archbishop's librarian came upon it and read it and soon after began to issue a series of pamphlets giving the Jesuit, Futurist view of prophecy. The idea soon found acceptance in the Anglo-Catholic Ritualistic movement in the National Church of England, and soon it tainted the very heart of Protestantism.

(b) The Secret Rapture doctrine was given a second door of entrance at this time by the ministry of one, Edward Irving, founder of the so-called *'Catholic Apostolic Church'*. It was in Irving's London church, in 1830, that a young girl named Margaret McDonald gave an ecstatic prophecy in which she claimed there would be a special secret coming of the Lord to *'rapture'* those awaiting His return. From then until his death in 1834 Irving devoted his considerable talent as a preacher to spreading the theory of the *'secret rapture'*.

(c) However, it was necessary for Jesuitry to have a third door of entrance to the Reformed fold and this they gained via a sincere Christian, J. N. Darby, generally regarded as the founder of the 'Brethren'. As an Anglican curate Darby attended a number of mysteriously organized meetings on Bible Prophecy at Powers court in Ireland, and at these gatherings he learned about the *'secret rapture'*. He carried the teaching into the Brethren and hence into the heart of Evangelicalism. With a new veneer of being scriptural the teaching spread and was later popularized in the notes of the Schofield Reference Bible.

So today the three measures of Roman leaven have corrupted the Prophetic teaching of almost all the Fundamentalist world. What might we say of the *'secret rapture'*, can any good thing come out of Rome?

EARLY YEARS

Margaret McDonald was born in 1815 and lived in Port Glasgow, Scotland during the beginning years of the Dispensationalism movement under John Nelson Darby. McDonald was fifteen years old in 1830 when she claimed to be a "prophetess." She would often go into trances and record visions of the end of the world. Not much is known about Margaret McDonald the individual, but history indicates that she perhaps had a larger influence on the early development of Dispensationalism than first suspected, and the controversy over her influence on the movement continues. Margaret was a member of Edward Irving's congregation and shared with him her visions of a secret rapture of the church. She also shared these same views with John Darby during a Darby visit of Port Glasgow. Irving proposed the new doctrine of a secret rapture of the church at a prophecy conference in Dublin Ireland in 1830 at Powers court Castle and soon after, Darby developed the full-fledged doctrine of Dispensationalism as it is known today. Among her prophecies, McDonald claimed that Robert Owen, the founder of New Harmony, Indiana was the Antichrist.

Critics of Dispensationalism have pointed out the fact that John Darby has based his own development of Dispensational theology on the prophetic visions of Margaret McDonald and her views of the pre-tribulation rapture.

THE WORD RAPTURE

The Rapture is a doctrine used by the Christian church to explain what will happen when Jesus Christ returns to save his church from the Great Tribulation. The word, "Rapture," is not found in the Old Testament or New Testament Scriptures, whether in the original languages, Hebrew, Greek, or English Bible translations.

The word 'rapture' itself is from the Latin *raptus,* and it connotes either apocalyptic spiritual overtones or possessive and physical undertones. The origin of rapture dates to the late 16th century, (directly or via French *rapere*) from Medieval Latin raptura "seizure," from the Latin cognate *raptus,* meaning, "seized and taken, kidnapped by force, snatched hold of and then taken hostage, carried off or away." In Medieval time, raptus was sometimes used to describe the euphoria soldiers experienced after defeating a foe in battle, then seizing the opponent, and taking him away as captive. Greek *raptus virginum Sabinarum* is a reference to the Sabine virgins, who were raped and abducted.

There is a literary connection between the words 'rapture' and 'rape.' To rape someone is to force somebody to have sex. Rape also implies the use of force to violate something, or to treat something in a violent, destructive, or abusive way (e.g. - Rape the land for its resources). During the brutal conquests of the 14th century, Anglo-Norman 'rapers' pillaged the land and people, and this term 'raper' meant to seize and carry off somebody or something by force (archaic). The word raper is directly from Latin rapere "to seize."

The use and meaning of the word 'rapture' has changed dramatically over time. Rapture is a noun that means:

1.   Overwhelming happiness: a euphoric transcendent state in which somebody is overwhelmed by happiness or delight and

unaware of anything else.

2.   In Christianity mystical transportation: a mystical experience of being transported into the spiritual realm, sometimes applied to the second coming of Jesus Christ when true believers are expected to rise up to join him in heaven.

If you are familiar with the Latin words used to describe a specific class of birds of prey, such as eagles or hawks, they are known as, "raptors," because of their method of hunting, which is to, "seize," live prey with their sharp, powerful talons, grasping rodents or fish *unaware* or hopelessly trying to escape, and then they, "carry it away." The raptor as a bird of prey is also from the 14th century Latin, "robber," which is also derived from the obsolete French word rapere.

The Latin Vulgate is the only translation of the Bible where you will find the word *rapture* in its Latin form. In the Latin Vulgate of 1st Thessalonians 4:17 we read:

4:17 deinde nos qui vivimus qui relinquimur simul **rapiemur** cum illis in nubibus obviam Domino in aera et sic semper cu*m Domino erimus.

While in the English translation we read the following:

"...then we that are alive, that are left, shall together with them be

caught up in the clouds, to meet the Lord in the air: and so shall we ever be with the Lord."* **(RSV Translation)**

The word that evolved into 'rapture' was 'rapiemur'. That's the first person plural, passive, of the verb 'rapio, rapere', which is translated as 'we....shall....be caught up...'

The parts of the verb are rapio, rapere, rapui, and raptus. Its meanings are 'drag off, snatch, destroy, seize, and carry off'. The future participle (English does not have an equivalent) is 'rapturus', one form of which is 'raptura'. The future participle translates roughly as 'about to carry off'. From 'raptura' it's a short jump to English 'rapture'.

The complete word study dictionary defines the Greek word for "caught up" this way:

αρπάζω

harpázo; fut. *harpáso*, aor. pass. *herpásthen*, 2d aor. pass. *herpágen*. To seize upon, spoil, snatch away. In Class. Gr., the fut. pass. *harpázomai* is used more often than in the NT. Literally, to seize upon with force, to rob; *differing from klépto (**G2813**), to steal secretly. It denotes an open act of violence in contrast to cunning and secret stealing.* **(The Complete Word Study Dictionary)**

1 Thessalonians 4:13-17 is describing the resurrection of the dead and not some secret rapture of the church. If you compare these

versus with 1 Corinthians 15:50-53, which is all about the resurrection of the dead, you will see that Paul is teaching believers to have a hope, not in a rapture, but in the resurrection.

(1 Th 4:13) *"And I do not wish you to be ignorant, brethren, concerning those who have **fallen asleep (the dead)**, that ye may not sorrow, as also the rest who have not hope,*

(1 Th 4:14) *for if we believe that Jesus died and **rose again (the resurrection)**, so also God those asleep through Jesus he will bring with him, **(those asleep are the dead with Jesus in heaven)***

(1 Th 4:15) *for this to you we say in the word of the Lord, that we who are living--who do remain over to the presence of the Lord-- may not precede those asleep,*

(1 Th 4:16) *because the Lord himself, in a shout, in the voice of a chief-messenger, and in the trump of God, shall come down from heaven and **the dead in Christ shall rise first (the resurrection)**,*

(1 Th 4:17) ***then we who are living**, who are remaining over, together with them **shall be caught away (the resurrection)** in clouds to meet the Lord in air, and so always with the Lord we shall be;"* **(Young's Literal Translation)**

(1 Co 15:51) *"lo, I tell you a secret; **we indeed shall not all sleep, and we all shall be changed (the resurrection)**;*

(1Co 15:52) *in a moment, in the twinkling of an eye,* **in the last trumpet, for it shall sound, and the dead shall be raised (the resurrection)** *incorruptible,* **and we--we shall be changed***:*

(1Co 15:53) *for it behoveth this corruptible to put on incorruption, and this mortal to put on immortality;"* **(Young's Literal Translation)**

This type of language is found in these passages and also in 1 Corinthians 15:20-24, 42-56. There is no rapture or secret rapture found anywhere in the OT or the NT only the resurrection of the dead. This type of Western Greco-Roman thinking has no foundation in the 1st century Jewish mind or teaching. The only teaching that is found in ancient Judaism before Messiah and at the time of Jesus is the resurrection of the dead.

THEN THE END

The apostle Paul when writing to the believers in Corinth explained to them the order of the resurrection and what would immediately take place after. In 1st Corinthians 15:20-24 we read the following:

(1Co 15:20) *"and now, Christ hath risen out of the dead--**the first-fruits** of those sleeping **(the dead)** he became,*

(1Co 15:21) *for since through man is the death, also through man is a rising again of the dead,* **(the resurrection of the dead)**
(1Co 15:22) *for even as in Adam all die, so also in the Christ all*

*shall be **made alive, (made alive through the resurrection of the dead)***

(1Co 15:23) *and each in **his proper order**, a first-fruit Christ, **afterwards** those who are the Christ's, in his presence,**(Christ was resurrected first then those who are believer's will be resurrected next)***

(1Co 15:24) ***then--the end, (the end is the resurrection)***

W.D. Davies (1948)

"('the end' in v. 24) "is a technical phrase denoting the final consummation immediately or at any rate with only a very short interval" (after the parousia). ***(Paul and Rabbinic Judaism, p. 295).***

Max King (1987)

"We need to give further attention to the meaning of "the end" and its connection with Christ's parousia. Much has been written about an interval of time between Christ's parousia (v.23) and "the end" (v.24) as implied in the temporal adverb "then" (*eita*). For those who see Christ's Messianic reign as occurring between His parousia and the end, a thousand-year interval is squeezed out of this temporal adverb." ***(The Cross and Parousia of Christ, p. 493)***

Complete Word Study Dictionary

télos; gen. *télous*, neut. noun. An end, term, termination,

completion. Particularly only in respect to time. In 1Co_15:24, the end of the work of redemption which is the entrance into heaven, the last or remainder of the dead in Christ. In an absolute sense, with *écho* (G2192), to have, to have an end means to be ended, figuratively to be destroyed.

A.T. Robertson

Then cometh the end (*eita to telos*). **No verb *ginetai*** in the Greek. Supply "at his coming," the end or consummation of the age or world.

There is no way around the fact that the resurrection of the dead is the final consummation of human history. When Jesus returns he will bring about the resurrection and judgment of the living and the dead. This verse demonstrates that first; Christ must be resurrected from the dead, and then at his coming all will be made alive. This is the order that Paul gives, then the end! Nothing else is covered except the fact that everything will be handed back to the father so that God will be all in all. This is a simple understanding of the text. Again, you will never find the word rapture in the original languages or a secret rapture being taught anywhere in the Bible. No such doctrine exists in Jewish history. The Jewish Encyclopedia says the following concerning the resurrection of the dead:

*"**It was believed that resurrection would occur at the close of the Messianic era** (Enoch, xcviii. 10, ciii. 8, civ. 5). This is particularly emphasized in II Esd. vii. 26-36: **"Death will befall the Messiah...,***

...Also, according to Syriac Apoc. Baruch (xxx. 1-5; l.-lii.; cxxxv. 15), **the resurrection will take place after the Messiah has "returned to heaven" and will include all men,** *the righteous to meet their reward, and the wicked to meet their eternal doom.* **This lasting doom is called "second death"** *(Targ. Deut. xxxiii. 6; Targ. Isa. xiv. 19; xxii. 14; lxv. 6, 15, 19; Jer. li. 39; Rev. xx. 6, 14)."*
(The Jewish Encyclopedia Online)

I am in no way saying that everything found in the Jewish Encyclopedia is 100% true but the fact the Messiah must die and return to heaven before the resurrection is to take place is found in the Jewish scripture themselves. The foundation of the Judeo Christian faith is the same.

THE JEWISH OLD TESTAMENT
In the literal sense of the word, resurrection refers to the event of a dead person completely returning to life. Thus it is not to be confused with things like Hellenistic immortality in which the soul continues to live after death, "free" of the body. Resurrection accounts are found in the Tanakh. The first five books of the Tanakh, known as the Torah, make some indications of an afterlife. For example, when Jacob dies, he says:

"I am about to be gathered to my kin. *Bury me with my forefathers in the cave which is in the field of Ephron the Hittite"*
(Genesis 49:29).

All the Jewish patriarchs and matriarchs (except Rachel) were buried in the family cave, and so were many other biblical personalities, including King Saul and King David. The Hebrew Bible refers to the term Sheol, which in traditional Judaism is translated simply as "grave" and is perceived as a transitory state.

Passages in the Hebrew Bible traditionally interpreted as referring to resurrection include: Ezekiel's vision of the valley of dry bones brought to restoration as a living army, which is commonly taken to be a metaphorical prophecy that the house of Israel would one day be gathered from the nations, out of exile, to live in the land of Israel once more and to an allusion to the resurrection of the dead:

*"He said to me, 'Prophesy to the breath, prophesy, son of man, and say to the breath, 'Thus says the Lord God, "Come from the four winds, O breath, and breathe on these slain, that they come to life.'"" So I prophesied as He commanded me, and the breath came into them, and they came to life, and stood on their feet, an exceedingly great army. Then He said to me, "Son of man, these bones are the whole house of Israel; behold, they say, 'Our bones are dried up, and our hope has perished. We are completely cut off.' "Therefore prophesy, and say to them, 'Thus says the Lord God, **"Behold, I will open your graves and cause you to come up out of your graves, My people; and I will bring you into the land of Israel."** (Ezekiel 37:9-12)*

Samuel - "The LORD kills and makes alive; He brings down to

Sheol and **rises up**." **(1 Samuel 2:6)**

Job - *"Even after my skin is destroyed,* ***Yet from my flesh*** *I shall see God"* **(Job 19:26)**

The book of Job is the oldest of all the Tanakh. It predates the Torah and all the Jewish writings. Before Moses wrote the first five books, Job had already written his book. The order the Tanakh is not the order of writings.

Isaiah - ***"Your dead will live; Their corpses will rise.*** *You who lie in the dust, awake and shout for joy, For your dew is as the dew of the dawn, And the earth will give birth to the departed spirits."* **(Isaiah 26:19)**

Daniel's vision, where a mysterious angelic figure tells Daniel, ***"Many of those who sleep in the dust of the ground will awake***, *these to everlasting life, but the others to disgrace and everlasting contempt."* **(Daniel 12:2)**

In the First Century BC, there were debates between the Pharisees who believed in the future Resurrection, and the Sadducees who did not. The Sadducees did not believe in an afterlife, but the Pharisees believed in a literal resurrection of the body. The Sadducees, politically powerful religious leaders, took a literal view of the Torah, rejecting the Pharisees' oral law, afterlife, angels, and demons. The Pharisees, whose views became Rabbinic Judaism, eventually won (or at least survived) this debate. The promise of a future resurrection appears in certain Jewish works, such as the Life of Adam and Eve, c 100 BC, and the Pharisaic book 2 Maccabees 7:14;23, c 124 BC.

The Old Testament Tanakh is the foundation of the teaching and belief of the universal resurrection of the dead and not rapture in which only the believers get taken and changed while everyone else who didn't believe in Jesus get left behind.

THE JEWISH NEW TESTAMENT

In John 5:28-29, the words of Jesus ring loud and clear in regards to when the final judgment will take place. This includes the resurrection of the dead, both for the righteous and the unrighteous.

(John 5:28) "*Do not marvel at this; for an hour is coming, in which **all who are in the tombs** will hear His voice,*

(John 5:29) ***and will come forth**; those who did the good deeds to a resurrection of life, those who committed the evil deeds to a resurrection of judgment.* "

Here is a commentary from A.T. Robertson on the above versus.

In the tombs (*en tois mnemeiois*). *Taphos* (grave) presents the notion of burial (*thapto*, to bury) as in Mat_23:27, *mnemeion* (from *mnaomai, mimnesko*, to remind) is a memorial (sepulchre as a monument). Jesus claims not only the power of life (spiritual) and of judgment, but of power to quicken the actual dead at **the Last Day**. They will hear his voice and come out (*ekporeusontai*, future middle indicative of *ekporeuomai*). **A general judgment and a general bodily resurrection we have here for both good and bad as in Mat_25:46**; Act_24:15; 2Co_5:10 and as often implied in the words of Jesus (Mat_5:29.; Mat_10:28; Luk_11:32). In Joh_6:39 Jesus asserts that he will raise up the righteous. **(A.T. Robertson Word Pictures of the New Testament)**

We must understand that Jesus is citing a passage in Daniel 12:2 where Daniel says:

*"Many of those who **sleep in the dust** of the ground **will awake, these to** everlasting life, **but the others** to disgrace and everlasting contempt."* **(Daniel 12:2)**

Another major verse in the gospel of John is found in chapter 11:22-24. Here we read that Martha came to Jesus after her brother Lazarus had dies four day earlier and said to him:

*"Lord, if you had been here, my brother would not have died. Even now I know that whatever you ask of God, God will give you." Then Jesus answered her and said, "Your brother will rise again." Martha said to him, "**I know that he will rise again in the resurrection on the last day.**"* **(John 11:22-24)**

Here we read that Martha understood completely about the resurrection of the dead on the last day. This was the Jewish understanding of what was to take place on the last day.

The apostle Paul followed the teaching and understanding of the resurrection of the dead since he himself was a Pharisee among Pharisee's and well educated above his fellows. Paul states in Acts 17:30-31 that God has fixed **a day** in which he will judge the world in righteousness through Jesus. He also told Timothy in 2 Timothy 4:1, *"I charge thee therefore before God, and the Lord Jesus Christ, who shall **judge the quick and the dead at his appearing** and his kingdom;*

The apostle Paul continues in front of the chief priests and all the council by declaring that he is on trial for the hope and resurrection of the dead not the rapture!(Acts 23:1-6) Again in Acts 24, before Felix, in versus 14 and 15 we read:

*" But this I confess unto thee, that after the way which they call heresy, so worship I the God of my fathers, believing all things which are written in the law and in the prophets: And have hope toward God, which they themselves also allow, **that there shall be a resurrection of the dead, both of the just and unjust.** "* **(Acts 23:1-6)**

Again A.T. Robertson points out the following;
Both of the just and the unjust (*dikaion te kai adikon*).
Apparently at the same time as in Joh_5:29 (cf. Act_17:31.) **(A.T.**

Robertson Word Picture of the New Testament)

Finally Paul is brought before Agrippa in Acts 26:1-8, where Paul is again standing on trial for the hope of the promise made by God to their forefathers and which the twelve tribes hoped to attain, namely the resurrection of the dead. This was a belief held by the Pharisee's and Rabbi's before and during the time of Christ, NOT some secret rapture! The resurrection of the dead was the final judgment at the Messiah's return, both for the righteous and the unrighteous.

THE MYSTERY OF THE RESURRECTION

A person asked me a question one day about the resurrection. They asked me what was going to happen to our bodies when Jesus returned. At that moment I thought of what the Apostle Paul said to the Corinthians in chapter 15 versus 51-53;

"Behold, I tell you a mystery; we will not all sleep, but we will all be changed, in a moment, in a twinkling of an eye, at the last trumpet; for the trumpet will sound, and the dead will be raised imperishable, and we will be changed. For this perishable must put on imperishable, and this mortal must put on immortality."

Paul refers to this change as a mystery (*musterion*). He does not claim that he has explained everything. He has drawn a broad parallel which opens the door of hope and confidence. The best way I can explain this change comes in the understanding of the spirit and the body now. Our body is described as a tent or a vessel animated by our spirit. When we die the spirit leaves the body and returns to the Lord (2Cor.5:6-9). But imagine when the spirit returns to the body at the resurrection, then what? Our spirit and body unit as one and we then have a spiritual body just like Jesus. Paul said that if there is a natural body then there is a spiritual body at the resurrection (1 Cor. 15:42-44). The key to understanding comes in the phrase *natural* and *spiritual*. We have a natural body on the outside and a spirit on the inside. Now think of the reverse at the resurrection. Our spirit now surrounds the outside of the body and now the body becomes glorified, immortal and imperishable. Remember the order, the *natural* body first, what we now live in, then the *spiritual* body at the resurrection. The mystery is how this is possible. Only God who is the creator and giver of life knows.

JESUS DIED

The fact that Jesus died on the cross is rarely argued. But there are some that claim that he didn't die on the cross but was revived by his disciples in the tomb. Let's examine the evidence for the death of Jesus. It begins with the fact that the gospels record that at the garden of Gethsemane Jesus was in agony and that he began to sweet great drops of blood. This is known in the medical field as hematidrosis. This happens under severe anxiety and stress. This also set up the skin to become extremely fragile. We must understand that Roman soldiers used a whip of braided leather thongs with metal balls woven into them. The balls would cause deep bruises or contusions, which would break open the skin with further blows. The whip also had pieces of sharp bones, which would cut or tare into the flesh severely. The whipping would have been from the upper to the lower parts of the body, front and back. The third-century historian named Eusebius described the flogging by saying, "The sufferer's veins were laid bare, and the very muscles, sinews, and bowels of the victim were open to exposure".

This is a very graphic image of a Roman flogging and a typical one. Most people died before they were crucified because of the flogging. The loss of blood would have been great. Jesus would have been in hypovolemic shock. This means that at the amount of blood loss the heart would race to try to pump blood that wasn't there. The blood pressure would drop causing fainting or collapse. The kidneys would stop producing urine to maintain what volume is left. Finally Jesus would become very thirsty as the body craves fluids to replace the lost blood volume. This is why Jesus is described as collapsing on the way to Calvary while carrying the horizontal beam of the cross. This is also why Jesus was thirsty while hanging on the cross. Jesus was in hypovolemic shock. The nails used were five to seven inches long and tapered to a sharp point. The nails were driven through the wrists and would go through the median nerves which are the largest nerves going out of the hands. The death on the cross was so indescribable that they had to invent a new word in order to describe the intense anguish that was caused during the crucifixion. The word was *excruciating* and literally means "out of the cross". Think about it, there was nothing in the language that would describe the intensity of a crucifixion. Also, we need to understand that Jesus was hanging in a vertical position, which is essentially an agonizing slow death by asphyxiation. Jesus would have also gone into respiratory acidosis leading to an irregular heartbeat. Jesus would have been aware of his moment of death. After Jesus died a Roman soldier put a spear through his side to confirm it. The criminals on the side of Jesus were not dead yet so the Roman soldiers broke their legs to speed up their death. The Romans were experts in the art of killing. There is no question that Jesus died on the cross even from a medical standpoint.

JESUS HAS RISEN

The next thing we must examine is whether or not Jesus was resurrected from the dead. Jesus himself made the claim in John chapter 2 verses 19-21 when he was in the temple. Jesus overturned the tables and the Jews asked him for a sign in order to show authority for doing so. Jesus answered in verse 19, ***"Destroy this temple, and in three days I will raise it up."*** John said in verse 21 that he was speaking of the temple of his body. It's interesting to note that the Greek word for body is *soma* and John used that word to describe a literal bodily resurrection. In Matthew chapter 16 verses 21-22 Jesus begins to tell his disciples that he must go to Jerusalem and suffer, be killed and be raised on the third day. If one compares the gospel accounts of the foretelling of Jesus' death and resurrection, it is clear that they all agree on the events.

Paul, who was a persecutor of the Christian church, witnessed and saw the resurrected Jesus on the road to Damascus. Paul became a believer very quickly and began to teach that Jesus was the Messiah and was killed and resurrected on the third day. In 1 Corinthians chapter 15 verses 14-17 Paul makes it very clear that if Christ did not rise from the dead then they're preaching and faith are empty or in vain.

All the gospels and letters of Paul and the Apostles teach that Jesus was raised from the dead. The empty tomb shows that the body is gone. If the body was stolen or put in another tomb then the Jews would have produced the body in order to show that the followers of Christ were wrong. Also there were soldiers guarding the tomb in order to prevent anyone from stealing the body. These Roman soldiers were trained in the art of killing and could not have been easily overtaken. The fact that the disciples were hiding until Christ appeared and then became mighty men, not afraid to die, shows that they had to have seen the risen Christ. When Christ appeared to the disciples in Luke 24 verses 36-42 he made it clear to them that he was not a spirit or a ghost but the risen Lord. Jesus said to them, *"Why are you troubled, and why do doubts arise in your hearts? See My hands and My feet, that it is I Myself; touch Me and see, for a spirit does not have flesh and bone as you see that I have."* He then ate with them as evidence of his resurrection. Again in John chapter 20 verses 24-29 Thomas would not believe unless he saw and handled for himself the risen Christ. Jesus then appeared to them in the upper room and said to Thomas, *"Reach here with your finger, and see My hands; and do not be unbelieving, but believe."* Thomas became a believer very quickly after that encounter, even calling him Lord and God. The whole idea of the resurrection is made very clear in the Bible and is at the heart of Christianity. Paul also records that there were over 500 eyewitnesses who had seen the risen Christ, (1 Cor.15: 3-8). This rules out the possibility of hallucination because people cannot share the same hallucination, especially 500+ eyewitnesses.

Jesus rising from the dead is very clear from a logical and rational standpoint. Christianity is what it is today because of this fact. The gospels state this and all the letters and creeds from the 1st century on support it. The point needs to be made clear that these men who witnessed the resurrection died for what they believed. It changed them from cowards to bold men who went out and preached the resurrection. Would you die for something you know to be a lie?

ERRORS IN ESCHATOLOGY

We must consider the fact that the Western view and understanding of eschatology has errors. When someone relies on the news to interpret and understand the Bible or news paper for that matter, errors will arise in the interpretation of Bible. The first major error in modern Western eschatology is the interpretation of Daniel 9:27. In one verse in Daniel 9 it is believed to say that the antichrist will make a 7 year peace agreement with Israel and then break it half way through. No where else in the entire Bible including the New Testament will you find such a verse or teaching. This is the only verse in the entire Jewish Bible that is used to teach such a thing. If Daniel 9:27 does not teach such a doctrine then the entire structure of dispensational eschatology collapses. Without the 7 year peace agreement with the antichrist there can be no 7 year tribulation or an antichrist for that matter. Does Daniel 9:27 teach such a doctrine? We must look at Daniel 9 not from the English translation but from the Hebrew language in which it was written in.

DANIEL 9

For years I have listened to prophecy teacher's talk about a 7 years peace agreement that the antichrist would make with Israel. Then in the middle of the peace agreement, he would break it and start the second half with great tribulation against the world. I never realized that this whole doctrine was based not the New Testament but only from a small part of a verse in the Old Testament. It is only found in Daniel 9:27. Every major so called prophecy teacher interprets the "He" in the beginning of the verse as the antichrist, even though it doesn't say antichrist in the entire passage. They even put in brackets "He (antichrist)" in their presentations. But if anyone looks at the Hebrew and Aramaic grammar of Daniel, they will find something totally different.

The goal of the seventy weeks as described in Daniel 9:24 is an ultimate age of fulfillment and completion. Its accomplishments are those found elsewhere in prophecies of God's new and everlasting covenant and of the eschatological jubilee. See, for example, Isaiah 60:21; 61:1 ft.; Jeremiah 31:34; 32:40; Ezekiel 16:60-63; 20:37f; 37:26. The final item listed in Daniel 9:24 is an anointing, which must surely be related to the anointed one of Daniel 9:25. Daniel 9:27. These are the elect within the covenant; cf. Daniel 11:33; 12:3.

The *antecedent* goes back to the proper noun Messiah in verse 26 not a people or a prince. The proper noun in Hebrew makes verse 27's "*he*" refers back to Messiah who will *confirm* NOT make the covenant. In Hebrew the proper noun is the Messiah not a people or a prince, which are all improper nouns with no definite article. Therefore the *antecedent* must go back to the proper noun, Messiah. It cannot be translated back to a people or even to a prince. The grammar forbids it!

Does the idea of confirming a covenant fit with Jesus Christ being the perpetrator of that confirmation? Yes! Jesus said, Mt 26:28 "This is my blood of the new testament [covenant], which is shed for many for the remission of sins." Heb 9:14, 15 "How much more shall the blood of Christ... purge your conscience from dead works to serve the living God? And for this cause he is the mediator of the New Testament" [covenant] "Testament" is translated from the same word in the Greek from which "covenant" is translated. Jesus is: Heb 8:6 ...mediator of the new **covenant**, Mal 3:1 ...messenger of the **covenant,** His shed blood is called: Heb 12:24 ...**the blood of the everlasting covenant** Jesus Christ confirmed the covenant through his redemptive sacrifice at Calvary.

In verse 27 of Daniel the rest of the verse should read as follows:

And he (Messiah) shall confirm the covenant with many for one week: and in the midst of the week he (Messiah) shall cause the sacrifice and the oblation to cease (In the Temple), and for the overspreading of abominations he (Messiah) shall make [The Temple] desolate, even until the consummation, and that determined (By Messiah) shall be poured upon the desolate (The Temple). **(Daniel 9:27; qbible.com)**

This is a more literal Hebrew translation of the text. This is exactly what Jesus prophesied concerning Israel and the Temple in Matthew 24, Mark 13 and Luke 21. To say that the *"he"* in Daniel 9:27 is the antichrist is to also say that the Messiah is the antichrist as well because according to the Hebrew grammar the *"he"* is the Messiah. Only a violation of the grammar and the text can you assume that Daniel is speaking about someone else other then the Messiah.

Here also are some historical and scholarly references to the seventy weeks of Daniel.

Josephus

"A sufficient proof of this is afforded by the passage, Josephus Arch. 10:1 1, 7, 'Daniel predicted also the Roman supremacy, and that our country should be desolated by them.'

The Targumim of the Megillot

(Lamentations 4) "17 Our eyes still fail to see our help *which we expected to come from the Romans, but which turned* to naught *for us.* In hope we watched for the *Edomites who were a* nation which could not save. 18 They prowled our paths so that we could not walk *safely* in our open places. *We said,* "Our end is near; our days are fulfilled," for our end had come." (**Targum Lamentations**)

Aquila

"On thy people, and on thy sacred city.. For ending disobedience, and for completing transgression. For the fulfilling of their disobedience and the completion of their sin, For the propitiation of their transgression, For the bringing in of everlasting righteousness, And for fulfilling the vision and the prophet. For the anointing of the most consecrated," (Quoted in **Demonstratio Evangelica (Proof of the Gospel) ; BOOK VIII**)

Josephus

"Daniel prophesied and wrote about all this many years ago. Similarly we can read in his writings about the way our people came under the yoke of Roman slavery and how our nation was destroyed by the Romans. All these writings Daniel left by God's command to give to the readers and students of history proof of the great honour God had granted him and to convince the doubters, who close out all possibility of guidance from life, that God still is concerned with the course of history." (Josephus, *Antiquities*, X.10 and 11.)

Rabbi Judah (Main Compiler of the Talmud)

"These times were over long ago" (Regarding Daniel's prophecy - Babylonian Talmud Sanhedrin 98b and 97a)

Rabbi Moses Abraham Levi

"I have examined and searched all the Holy Scriptures and have not found the time for the coming of Messiah clearly fixed, except in the words of Gabriel to the prophet Daniel, which are written in the 9th chapter of the prophecy of Daniel."

Africanus (160-240)

"The section thus expressed gives much strange information. But here I will make the necessary examination of the times and the matters connected with them. It is clear, then, that the coming of the

Christ is foretold as to occur after seventy weeks. For in the time of our Saviour, or after His time, sins are done away and transgressions ended. And by this remission iniquities are blotted out (c) by a propitiation together with unrighteousness, eternal righteousness is published beyond that of the law, visions and prophecies (last) until John, and the Holy of holies is anointed. For these things existed in expectation only before our Saviour's Coming. And the angel explains we must count the numbers, that is to say the seventy weeks, which are 490 years, from the going forth of the word of answer and from the building of Jerusalem. This took place in the twentieth year of Artaxerxes, King of Persia. For Nehemiah his cup-bearer made the request, (d) and received the answer that Jerusalem should be rebuilt, and the order went forth to carry it out. For till that date the city lay desolate. For when Cyrus after the seventieth year of the Captivity spontaneously allowed everyone who wished to return, those with Joshua the High Priest and Zerubbabel went back, and those afterwards with Ezra, and were at first prevented from building the Temple, and the wall of the City, as no order had been given for it; and so |125 there was a delay until Nehemiah and the reign of Artaxerxes and the one hundred and fifteenth year of the Persian Empire. And this was 185 years from the taking of Jerusalem. It was then that King Artaxerxes gave the order (390) for it to be built. And Nehemiah was sent to take charge of the work, and the street and wall were built, as it had been prophesied. And from that date to the coming of Christ is seventy weeks. For if we begin to count from any other point but this, not only the dates will not agree, but many absurdities arise. If, for instance, we begin counting the seventy weeks from Cyrus and the first Mission, the period will be too long by more than a century, if from (b) the day the angel prophesied to Daniel still longer, and longer still if we start from the beginning of the Captivity. For we find the length of the Persian Empire to be 230 years, and of the Macedonian 300, and from then to the sixteenth year of Tiberius Caesar 60 years. And from Artaxerxes to the time of Christ seventy weeks are (c) completed according to Jewish reckoning. For from Nehemiah, who was sent by Artaxerxes to rebuild Jerusalem, in the one hundred and fifteenth year of the Persian Empire, and in the twentieth year of Artaxerxes, and in the fourth year of the eighty-third Olympiad up to that date, which was the second year of the two hundred and second Olympiad, and the sixteenth year of the reign of Tiberius Caesar, there are 475 years, or 490 according to Hebrew reckoning. For they reckon years by the course of the moon, I ought to (d) tell you, counting 354 days, while the course of the sun is 365 ¼ days, twelve lunar revolutions, being exceeded by one solar by 11¼ days. Therefore the Greeks and the Jews add three intercalary months to every eighth year. For eight times 11¼ days makes three months. So then 465 years, in eight-year cycles, makes fifty-nine years and three months. Since adding the three intercalary months every eighth year, we have a few days short of fifteen years. And these added (391) to the 475 years complete the seventy weeks." (Fifth Book of his *Chronography,* Quoted in **Demonstratio Evangelica (Proof of the Gospel) ; BOOK VIII***)*

St. Augustine

"For let us not suppose that the computation of Daniel's weeks was interfered with by this shortening of those days, or that they were not already at that time complete, but had to be completed afterwards in the end of all things, for Luke most plainly testifies that the prophecy of Daniel was accomplished at the time when Jerusalem was overthrown." (Matt. 24:22, *Golden Chain*)

Barnabus

"This abstract discussion of Judaism is the sign of an epoch when the Judaizing controversies were already a thing of the past in the main body of the Church. In settling the date of the letter reference is often made to verses 3-5 of chapter four, where the writer, it is believed, finds the fulfilment of the prophecy of Daniel (Dan. 7:7, sqq.) in the succession of the Roman Emperors of his time." (**New Advent Catholic Encyclopedia**)

Clement of Alexandria (150-215)

"And thus Christ became King of the Jews, reigning in Jerusalem in the fulfillment of the seven weeks. And in the sixty and two weeks the whole of Judaea was quiet, and without wars. And Christ our Lord, "the Holy of Holies," having come and fulfilled the vision and the prophecy, was anointed in His flesh by the Holy Spirit of His Father. In those "sixty and two weeks," as the prophet said, and "in the one week," was He Lord. The half of the week Nero held sway, and in the holy city Jerusalem placed the abomination; and in the half of the week he was taken away, and Otho, and Galba, and

Vitellius. And Vespasian rose to the supreme power, and destroyed Jerusalem, and desolated the holy place." (*Miscellanies*) "The half of the week Nero held sway, and in the holy city Jerusalem placed the abomination; and in the half of the week he was taken away, and Otho, and Galba, and Vitellius. And Vespasian rose to the supreme power, and destroyed Jerusalem, and desolated the holy place. And that such are the facts of the case, is clear to him that is able to understand, as the prophet (i.e., Daniel) said." (*Miscellanies* 1:21)

Eusebius (314)

"And all these things were fulfilled when the seventy weeks were completed at the date of our Saviour's Coming." "I think that the fact that the intermediate period of their primacy, during which they governed, is meant, is shewn by the words, "From the going forth of the answering and the building of Jerusalem, until Christ the governor, is seven weeks and sixty-two weeks." And the weeks of years make 483 years added together from the reign of Cyrus up to the Roman Empire, when Pompeius (392) the Roman general attacked Jerusalem and took the city by siege, and the whole city became subject to Rome, so that thenceforward it paid taxes, and obeyed the Roman enactments."

(c) "20. AND while I yet spake and prayed and confessed my sins and the sins of my people Israel, and casting my misery before the holy Mount of my God, 21. and while I yet spake in prayer, behold the man Gabriel, whom I had seen at the beginning came flying, and he touched me about the time of the evening sacrifice. 22. And he instructed me and spake with me, saying, O (d) Daniel, 23. I am now come forth to impart to thee understanding. At the beginning of thy supplication the word came forth, and I am come to tell thee, for thou art a man greatly beloved: therefore consider the matter, understand the vision, for thou art a man greatly beloved. 24. Seventy weeks have been decided on for thy people, and for the holy city, for sin to be ended, and to seal up transgressions, and to blot out iniquities, and to make atonement for iniquities, and to bring in everlasting righteousness, and to seal the vision and the prophecy, and to anoint the Most Holy. 25. And thou shalt know and understand, that from the going forth of the command for the answer and for the building of Jerusalem until Christ the Prince shall be seven (382) weeks, and sixty-two weeks; and then it shall return, and the street shall be built, and the wall, and the times shall be exhausted. 26. And after the sixty-two weeks, the Anointing shall be destroyed, and there is no judgment in him, and he shall destroy the city and the sanctuary together with the coming prince; they shall be cut off in a flood, and, to the end of the war which is rapidly completed, in desolations. 27. And one week shall establish the covenant with many: and in the midst of the week my sacrifice and drink-offering shall be taken away: and on the temple shall be an (b) abomination of desolations: and at the end of time shall an end be put to the desolation." When the captivity of the Jewish people at Babylon was near its end, the Archangel Gabriel, one of the holy ministers of God, appeared to Daniel as he prayed, and told him that the restoration of Jerusalem was to follow without the slightest delay, and he defines the period after the restoration by numbering the years, and foretells that after the predetermined time it will again be destroyed, and that after the second capture and siege it will no longer have (c) God for its guardian, but will remain desolate, with the worship of the Mosaic Law taken away from it, and another new Covenant with humanity introduced in its place. This was what the Angel Gabriel revealed to the prophet as by secret oracles. So then he says to Daniel" Instead of, "For sin to be ended, and to seal up transgressions," Aquila translated, "For ending disobedience, and for completing transgression." I think that our Saviour's words to the Jews, "Ye have filled up the measure of your fathers," are parallel to this."

"And the people of the governor that cometh will destroy the city and the holy place." Meaning that the city and the Holy Place arc not only to be ruined by the leader to come, whom I have identified in my interpretation, but also by his people. And you would not be far wrong in saying, too, that the Roman general and his army arc meant by the words before us, where I think the camps of the Roman rulers are meant, who governed the nation from that time, and who destroyed the city of Jerusalem itself, and its ancient venerable Temple. For they were cut off by them as by a flood, and were at once involved in destruction until the war was concluded, so that the prophecy was fulfilled and they suffered utter desolation (400) after their plot against our Savior, which was followed by their extreme sufferings during the siege. You will find an accurate account of it in the history of Josephus." "But after the prophecy of the events that happened to the Jewish nation in the intermediate period between the |135 seven and sixty-two weeks, there follows the prophecy of the new Covenant announced by our Saviour. So when all the intermediate matter between the seven and the sixty-two weeks is finished, there is added, "And he will confirm (b) a Covenant with many one week," and in half the week the sacrifice and the libation shall be taken away, and on the Holy Place shall come the abomination of desolation, and until the fullness of time fullness shall be given to the desolation. Let us consider how this was fulfilled." (**Demonstratio Evangelica (Proof of the Gospel) ; BOOK VIII)**

Origen (2nd Century)

"The weeks of years, also, which the prophet Daniel had predicted, extending to the leadership of Christ, have been fulfilled" (*Principles*, 4:1:5).

Sulpicius Severus (403)

"But from the restoration of the temple to its destruction, which was completed by Titus under Vespasian, when Augustus was consul, there was a period of four hundred and eighty-three years. That was formerly predicted by Daniel, who announced that from the restoration of the temple to its overthrow there would elapse seventy and nine weeks. Now, from the date of the captivity of the Jews until the time of the restoration of the city, there were two hundred and sixty years. (p. 254, ch. 11)

Symmachus The Ebionite (161-80)

"Against thy people, and thy holy city"

Theodoret (430)

(Closes the period three years and a half after the suffering of Christ) "and so they begin the last week at the baptism of Christ" (Quoted by Willet)

F.F. Bruce (1971)

"When the temple area was taken by the Romans, and the sanctuary itself was still burning, the soldiers brought their legionary standards into the sacred precincts, set them up opposite the eastern gate, and offered sacrifice to them there, acclaiming Titus as **imperator** (victorious commander) as they did so. The Roman custom of offering sacrifice to their standards had already been commented on by a Jewish writer as a symptom of their pagan arrogance, but the offering of such sacrifice in the temple court was the supreme insult to the God of Israel. This action, following as it did the cessation of the daily sacrifice three weeks earlier, must have sensed to many Jews, as it evidently did to Josephus, a new and final fulfillment of Daniel's vision of a time when the continual burnt offering would be taken away and the abomination of desolation set up" (**Bruce**, p. 224)

Gary DeMar

"Dispensationalists need a gap between the feet and the toes of Nebuchadnezzar's statue.." (*Last Days Madness,* p. 172)

William Hales (1747-1831)

"And after the sixty and two weeks, before specified, as the largest division of the 70, was the anointed [leader] cut off judicially, by an iniquitous sentence, in the midst of the one week, which formed the third and last division, and began with our Lord's Baptism, about A.D. 27.--'when he was beginning to be thirty years of age,' and commenced his mission, which lasted three years and half until his crucifixion, about A.D. 31. "27. During this one week, which ended about A.D. 34 (about the martyrdom of Stephen,) a new covenant was established with many of the Jews, of every class; in the midst of which the Temple sacrifice was virtually abrogated by the all-sufficient sacrifice of the Lamb of God that taketh away the sins of the [repentant and believing] world."

Ernst Hengstenberg

"it was then regarded by the Jews as relating to a still future occurrence -- the yet impending conquest and destruction of Jerusalem." (Com. 2, page 584)

Keil and Delitzsch Commentary

"the interpretations may be divided into three principal classes. 1. Most of the church fathers and the older orthodox interpreters find prophesied here the appearance of Christ in the flesh, His death, and the destruction of Jerusalem by the Romans. 2. The majority of the modern interpreters, on the other hand, refer the whole passage to the time of Antiochus Epiphanes. 3. Finally, some of the church fathers and several modern theologians have interpreted the prophecy eschatologically, as an announcement of the development of the kingdom of God from the end of the Exile on to the perfecting of the kingdom by the second coming of Christ at the end of the days." (*Daniel*, p. 336)

J. Marcellus Kik

"The only valid objection against this general interpretation is that the destruction of Jerusalem did not occur within the seventieth week - within the period of seven years. The seventy weeks extended to about 33 A.D. The destruction of Jerusalem, of course, came in 70 A.D. A close examination of the passage in Daniel does not disclose any definite statement that the people of the prince were to cause this destruction within the seven years. Within the seven years the destruction of the city *was determined* by its rejection of Christ and his apostles. Because of that rejection the people of the prince that shall come shall destroy the city and the sanctuary." (*An Eschatology of Victory* 109-110)

"If the seventieth week were postponed we would still be in our sins!" (*An Eschatology of Victory* 108)

Samuel Lee (1849)

"The wording of the Hebrew is peculiar here and highly deserving of remark. It stands literally thus, — "Until (the) evening (and) morning, or it may be until the evening of the morning, two thousand and three hundred, and the sanctuary (lit. holiness) shall be sanctified." Evening and morning, I take here to be a mere periphrasis for a day; and so our translators have taken it, Genesis 1:5. The day here had in view must mark the period of Daniel's seventieth week — the numbers given above must be understood indefinitely, and as intended to designate a considerable length of time. This consummation could not be effected by Antiochus Epiphanes: he only suspended the service of the Temple for about three years and a half. By every consideration, therefore, it is evident that the Little Horn of Daniel's seventh and eighth chapters, is identically the same, and that this symbolized that system of *Roman rule* which ruined Jerusalem, and then made war upon the sainted servants and followers of the Son of man; and in this he prospered and practiced, until he in his turn fell, as did his predecessors, to rise no more at all. (An Inquiry into the Nature, Progress, and End of Prophecy, p. 168.)

John Lightfoot (1654)

"Daniel knowing from Jeremies Prophecie, that the seventy years of Captivity were now fully expired, addresseth himself to God by prayer for their return: he receiveth not only a gracious answer to his desire, but a Prediction of what times should pass over his people till the death of Christ; namely, seventy weeks, or seventy times seven years, or four hundred and ninety. This space of time the Angel divideth into three unequal parts.

1. Seven sevens, or forty nine years, to the finishing of Jerusalems Walls.

2. Sixty two sevens, or four hundred thirty four years, from that time, till the last seven.

3. The last seven in the latter half of which Christ Preacheth, viz. three years and a half, and then dieth, &c. The twenty seventh Verse therefore is to be read thus: He shall confirm the covenant with

many in the one week, and in half that week he shall cause Sacrifice and Oblation to cease, &c. So that from this year to the death of Christ are four hundred ninety years; and there is no cause, because of doubtful Records among the Heathen, to make a doubt of the fixedness of this time, which an Angel of the Lord hath pointed out with so much exactness." (Works, 1st. Ed., Vol. 1; Chronology, p. 136) "[C]hrist now hath three years and a half to live, and to be a publick Minister of the Gospel, as the angel Gabriel had told, Dan. 9.27. that in half of the last sevens of the years there named, he should confirm the Covenant: R. Jochanan saith, Three years and an half the Divine Glory stood upon the Mount of Olives and cried, Seek the Lord while he may be found. Midr. Till. fol. 10. col. 4." (Works, 1st. Ed., Vol. 1; Harmony, p. 10)

Philip Mauro (1925)

"We understand that the sense in which the death of Christ made an end of sins was that thereby he made a perfect atonement for sins, as written in Hebrews 1:3, 'when He had by Himself *purged our sin*,' and in many like passages." (*The Seventy Week*, p 47)

Jim McGuiggan (1978)

"When these 'seventy weeks' have 'run their course' God will have finished *altogether* his work with the Jews as a (Mosaic) commonwealth!" (*The Book of Daniel*, p. 151)

Isaac Newton (1642-1727)

"And in half a week he shall cause the sacrifice and oblation to cease; that is, by the war of the Romans upon the Jews: which war, after some commotions, began in the 13th year of Nero , A.D. 67, in the Spring when Vespasian with an army invaded them; and ended in the second year of Vespasian, A.D. 70, in autumn, September 7 when Titus took the city, having burnt the Temple 27 days before: so that it lasted three years and an half." "Thus have we in this short Prophecy, a prediction of all the main periods relating to the coming of the Messiah; the time of his birth, that of his death, that of the rejection of the Jews, the duration of the Jewish war whereby he caused the city and the sanctuary to be destroyed, and the time of his second coming: and so the interpretation here given is more full and complete and adequate to the design, than if we should restrain it to his first coming only, as Interpreters usually do. We avoid also the doing violence to the language of Daniel, by taking the 7 weeks and 62 weeks for one number. Had that been Daniel's meaning, he would have said sixty and nine weeks, and not seven weeks and sixty two weeks, a way of numbering used by no nation."

Blaise Pascal

"709. One must be bold to predict the same thing in so many ways. It was necessary that the four idolatrous or pagan monarchies, the end of the kingdom of Judah, and the seventy weeks, should happen at the same time, and all this before the second temple was destroyed. (**SECTION XI**) 722 (cont.). Daniel 9:20. "Whilst I was praying with all my heart, and confessing my sin and the sin of all my people, and prostrating myself before my God, even Gabriel, whom I had seen in the vision at the beginning, came to me and touched me about the time of the evening oblation, and he informed me and said, O Daniel, I am now come forth to give thee the knowledge of things. At the beginning of thy supplications I came to shew that which thou didst desire, for thou are greatly beloved: therefore understand the matter, and consider the vision. Seventy weeks are determined upon thy people, and upon thy holy city, to finish the transgression, and to make an end of sins, and to abolish iniquity, and to bring in everlasting righteousness; to accomplish the vision and the prophecies, and to anoint the Most Holy. (After which this people shall be no more thy people, nor this city the holy city. The times of wrath shall be passed, and the years of grace shall come forever.) "The street shall be built again, and the wall, even in troublous times. And after three score and two weeks," (which have followed the first seven. Christ will then be killed after the sixty-nine weeks, that is to say, in the last week), "the Christ shall be cut off, and a people of the prince that shall come shall destroy the city and the sanctuary, and overwhelm all, and the end of that war shall accomplish the desolation." (**SECTION XI**) 724. Predictions.--That in the fourth monarchy, before the destruction of the second temple, before the dominion of the Jews was taken away, in the seventieth week of Daniel, during the continuance of the second temple, the heathen should be instructed, and brought to the knowledge of the God worshipped by the Jews; that those who loved Him should be delivered from their enemies, and filled with His fear and love. And it happened that in the fourth monarchy, before the destruction of the second temple, etc., the heathen in great number worshipped God, and led an angelic life. (**SECTION XI**)

William Whiston (1737)

"This is a very remarkable day indeed, the seventeenth of Panemus, [Tammuz,] A.D. 70, when, according to Daniel's prediction, 606 years before, the Romans "In half a week caused the sacrifice and oblation to cease," Dan. ix. 27; for from the month of February, A.D. 66, about which time Vespasian entered on this war, to this very time, was just three years and a half.

"How general the reference of the prophecy then was to a future destruction of the city, appears from the express observation of Josephus, that even the zealots had no doubt of the correctness of this interpretation. The same interpretation is found also in the Babylonian and Jerusalem *Gemarah.*" (P. 215.)

"See Bishop Lloyd's Tables of Chronology, published by Mr. Marshall, on this year. Nor is it to be omitted, what year nearly confirms this duration of the war, that four years before the war begun was somewhat above seven years five months before the destruction of Jerusalem, ch. 5. sect. 3." (***Wars of the Jews*, VI,II,1**)

Zonaras (11/12th C.)

"commences the period at the 20th year of Artaxerxes Longimanus, and ends the 62 weeks at the death of Hyrcanus. From this point to Christ's baptism they reckon seven weeks more, and then in the midst of the last week, Messiah was slain; so there remained afterwards three years and a half for the preaching of the Gospel. *Eusebius* begins the 69 weeks in the sixth year of Darius Itystaspes, and ends them in the first year of Herod, about the death of Hyrcanus. He begins the 70th week at Christ's baptism, and ends the period three years and a half afterwards. *Tertullian,* by beginning in the first year of Darius, counts 490 years, to the destruction of Jerusalem." (**Dissertations on Calvin**) "The Covenant of the Seventieth Week" in The Law and the Prophets: Old Testament Studies in Honor of Oswald T. Allis, ed. by J.H. Skilton. [Nutley, NJ]: Presbyterian and Reformed, 1974, pp. 452-469.

From the scriptures, to the references listed above, we can see that the stories of dispensationalists just keep on growing. Can we really trust these men who will not submit themselves to the Bible even if it means that they are wrong? What are they afraid of? Losing their ministry? It is a hundred million dollar ministry for them. Is it really about the truth or just about money? You decide.

THE MARK OF THE BEAST?

We have heard of the stories of the coming mark of the beast which was the mark of the antichrist. This mark was to be placed on the people who were left behind from the rapture. This mark would allow them to buy and sell and without it you could be killed for not taking it. What is the mark of the best and who is the beast that is suppose to enforce this mark?

THE DISCOVERY

A fragment from the oldest surviving copy of the New Testament shows that the number of the Beast of Revelation 13 is 616. Ellen Aitken, a professor of early Christian history at McGill University, states that "the majority opinion seems to be that it refers to [the Roman emperor] Nero. The early fragment supports the view that Revelation was written prior to the destruction of Jerusalem in A.D. 70, and whether the number is 666 or 616, the number is a reference to Nero and not some end-time antichrist figure. Only time will tell how this discovery will affect dispensationalism.

The first readers of Revelation were told to "calculate the number of the Beast, for the number is that of a man; and his number is six hundred and sixty-six"(13:18). Since Revelation was written to a first-century audience, we should expect the first-century readers to be able to calculate the number with relative ease and understand the result. They would have had few candidates from which to choose. Notice that the number is "six hundred and sixty-six, not three sixes." Tim LaHaye misidentifies the number when he writes, "The plain sense of Scripture tells us that it comprises the numbers: six, six, six." The three Greek letters that make up the number represent 600, 60, and 6.

Ancient numbering systems used an alpha-numeric method. This is true of the Latin (Roman) system that is still common today: I=1, V=5, X=10, L=50, C=100, D=500, M=1000. Greek and Hebrew follow a similar method where each letter of their alphabets represents a number. The first nine letters represent 1 -9 while the tenth letter represents 10, with the nineteenth letter representing 100 and so on. Since the Book of Revelation is written in a Hebrew context by a Jew with numerous allusions to the Old Testament, we should expect the solution to deciphering the meaning of six hundred and sixty-six to be Hebraic. *"The reason clearly is that, while [John] writes in Greek, he thinks in Hebrew, and the thought has naturally affected the vehicle of expression."*

When Nero Caesar's name is transliterated into Hebrew, which a first-century Jew would probably have done, he would have gotten *Neron Kesar* or simply *nrwn qsr*, since Hebrew has no letters to represent vowels. "It has been documented by archaeological finds that a first century Hebrew spelling of Nero's name provides us with precisely the value of 666. Jastrow's lexicon of the Talmud contains this very spelling." When we take the letters of Nero's name and spell them in Hebrew, we get the following numeric values: n=50, r=200, w=6, n=50, q=100, s=60, r=200 = 666. "Every Jewish reader, of course, saw that the Beast was a symbol of Nero. And both Jews and Christians regarded Nero as also having close affinities with the serpent or dragon. . . . The Apostle writing as a Hebrew was evidently thinking as a Hebrew. . . . Accordingly, the Jewish Christian would have tried the name as he *thought* of the name - that is in *Hebrew letters*. And the moment that he did this the secret stood revealed. No Jew ever thought of Nero except as "*Neron Kesar*."

The fragment supports the reading of some Greek New Testament manuscripts that read 616 instead of 666. Why would someone making a copy of the Revelation scroll make such a number change? "Perhaps the change was intentional, seeing that the Greek form Neron Caesar written in Hebrew characters (*nrwn qsr*) is equivalent to 666, whereas the Latin forms Nero Caesar (*nrw qsr*) is equivalent to 616." A Latin copyist might have thought that 666 was an error because Nero Caesar did not add up to 666 when transliterated into Latin. He then changed 666 to 616 to conform to the Latin rendering since it was generally accepted that Nero was the Beast. In either case, a Hebrew transliteration nets 666, while a Latin spelling nets 616. Nero was the "man" and either 666 or 616 was his number.

The beast in Revelation was known to the first-century Jews as Nero and not some future antichrist who is never identified as such. We must stick with the scriptures and not man made stories that have no historical evidence but just wild assumptions to fit their belief and doctrine.

NO ANTICHRIST?

Once again we deal with the fact that the New Testament does not teach about a one man world leader on the rise who is called the antichrist. John is the only person who refers to an antichrist but not a one man world leader antichrist. The Greek word *"antichrist"* is a Greek adjective not a noun. In Hebrew it is *"anti-messiah"* and it refers and describes anyone who denies that Jesus came in the flesh or to anyone who just denies him. That person is the antichrist. John tells you who the antichrist is, so stop trying to guess what the scriptures all ready teach.

*"For many deceivers have gone out into the world, those who do not acknowledge Jesus Christ as coming in the flesh. **This is the deceiver and the antichrist.**"* (**1John 2:18-22; 2John 1:7**).

We have been guessing for years. Listed below are several world figures that have been tagged as the Antichrist. Most of these men are dead and presumably off the hook, but a number of them are still active on the so called world stage.

Antiochus Epiphanes He was one of only a few pre-Christ candidates and is described by scholars as being a type of Antichrist. Epiphanes was predicted by Daniel the prophet, and he fulfilled many of the prophecies.

Roman Emperor Nero He was one of the first and one of the greatest persons to fit the role of Antichrist. He put many Christians to death, and even killed members of his own family. Nero's actions actually helped the Church to multiply faster. When he learned the Roman Senate was plotting against him, he died by his own hand and sword.

The Pope Just about every pope has been given the title of Antichrist. The pontiff is a favorite among evangelicals. During the Middle Ages, when the power of the pope was more pronounced, the title was more plausible. Today, the political power of the Pope has long since waned.

Charlemagne He lived from 742-814 AD and controlled much of Central Europe. Charlemagne put himself into the shoes of the Antichrist by trying to rebuild the Roman Empire, a task that only the real Antichrist will accomplish. He died before achieving his goal.

Napoleon The self-crowned French Emperor was not particularly a depraved man: He did not persecute the Church, and he lacked a number of the qualities needed for the role. His downfall was that he loved war too much. Napoleon, like Charlemagne, worked at reviving the Roman Empire.

Aleister Crowley He was a male witch who lived in England from 1875 to 1947, and who was so evil that his nicknames were "the Beast" and "666." A number of rock and roll groups such as The Beatles, The Doors and Ozzy Osbourne featured references to him on their albums.

Franklin Delano Roosevelt The numerical value of FDR's name was reported to add up to 666. Because of the Great Depression, FDR was the most autocratic US President of the 20th century. Roosevelt was in office for 12 years.

Benito Mussolini Because Mussolini became the dictator of Italy, the original capital of the Roman Empire, he was the subject of a great deal of commentary during his rule from 1922 to 1943. His extreme arrogance fit the role of Antichrist, but his military capabilities were laughable. Italy needed help from Germany all throughout World War II.

Adolf Hitler Most people would describe this man as the most villainous man who ever lived. He remains a demonic forewarning.

Joseph Stalin This Russian dictator is believed to be the greatest mass murderer of all time, having killed 30 million people. Most of history's tyrants killed foreigners; Stalin specialized in killing his own citizens.

Francisco Franco He was the dictator of Spain from 1936 until his death in 1975. Franco was called the Antichrist not because of his actions, but more because of a genealogical connection. Upon his death, the dubious honor of being called the Antichrist passed to Prince Juan Carlos.

John F. Kennedy As the nation's first Roman Catholic President, John F. Kennedy was believed to do the pope's bidding. At the 1956 Democratic convention, he received 666 votes. When Kennedy was shot dead in Dallas, several people waited for this deadly wound to heal. It never happened.

Henry Kissinger Because of Mr. Kissinger's activity in the Middle East, he was labeled the Antichrist. I've always thought his raspy voice would be the first thing to disqualify him.

King Juan Carlos of Spain The late prophecy teacher Charles Taylor was a big proponent of the idea that Juan Carlos is the Antichrist because of his bloodline and because he's the king of the tenth nation to join the European Union.

Ayatollah Khomeini One of the grumpiest men to ever live, he bedeviled the US for a number of years.

Ronald Wilson Reagan Say it isn't so, Ron. During the '80s when he was President, there was talk going around about the fact that he had six letters in all three of his names.

Mikhail Gorbachev The first Russian leader to support the rights of the people has been and remains a candidate for the job of Antichrist. Until Gorby dies, prophecy watchers will keep an eye on him. I guess being born with that mark on his head was too obvious for some.

Maitreya A camera-shy New Age personage, who is said to be on this earth somewhere, is waiting for his opportunity to save the world.

Sun Myung Moon This leader of the Unification Church openly claims to be the Messiah. Moon recently was sent to jail for tax evasion. Jesus, by having a tax collector on His staff, didn't suffer from tax problems. You pick which one was the smarter Messiah.

PLO leader Yassir Arafat When Arafat signed the peace treaty with Israel in 1993, some thought that he was bringing to pass the prophecy regarding the Antichrist signing a seven-year peace treaty with Israel. In order for this to be the case, we would be well into the tribulation period.

Louis Farrakhan Farrakhan has worked hard to earn the title of Antichrist: He has met with every Islamic dictator there is, and he's called the Jewish faith "a gutter religion." Farrakhan has said that Jesus was "just a prophet" and that he, Louis Farrakhan, is the true Jesus.

Karl Hapsburg Just like Juan Carlos, Karl Hapsburg has a good shot at being the Antichrist simply because of who he is. His family holds the title of ruler over Jerusalem. The Hapsburg family also reigned over the Holy Roman Empire at one time. The European Union will be a revival of the Roman Empire.

William Jefferson Clinton A number of folks have e-mailed me saying, "Clinton is Satan's pet." I came across information posted in newsgroups and websites that add up William Jefferson Clinton numerologically to total 666.

Sam Donaldson of ABC News So many people have submitted Donaldson's name that I finally decided to add him to the list. By including Sam, I hope I don't cause any jealousy at ABC News.

Barney the Dinosaur Because John, the writer of Revelation, would never have known what a dinosaur looked like, it's logical to assume he would have identified any vision of Barney as one of a dragon. Taking this into consideration, you might find the following Scriptures quite revealing: Revelation 12:3, "And there appeared another wonder in heaven; and behold a great red dragon...," Revelation 13:4, "And they worshipped the dragon which gave power unto the beast: and they worshipped the beast, saying, who is like unto the beast? who is able to make war with him?" Revelation 20:2, "And he laid hold on the dragon, that old serpent, which is the Devil, and Satan, and bound him a thousand years."

Bill Gates If the beast needs to be computer literate and financially well-off, then Bill Gates is a good candidate.

Prince Charles of Wales I'm told that Prince Charles could be the beast. Charles has had the familiar numerology claims made about him--ones that equate his name with 666. Further, he is believed to have ancestral links to the Roman Empire. It was also reported to me that he's a vegetarian, which could explain why the Antichrist will stop the daily animal sacrifices in the Jewish Temple.

Jacques Chirac French President Jacques Chirac has been involved in a flurry of diplomatic activity. His high profile has caught the attention of several prophecy watchers.

These men have been branded in their life time as being the antichrist. Every generation has a so called candidate for being the antichrist. The guessing needs to stop. Let's get back to the Jewish scriptures and study what God has to say to us.

THE OLIVET DISCOURSES

When considering the gospel's for understanding eschatology we must first understand their background. For example, Matthew was written originally in Hebrew to the Jews. This is established by the early church fathers who wrote the following:

Papias (150-170 CE) - Matthew composed the words in the Hebrew dialect, and each translated as he was able. [A quote by Eusebius; Eccl. Hist. 3:39]

Ireneus (170 CE) - Matthew also issued a written Gospel among the Hebrews in their own dialect. [Against Heresies 3:1]

Origen (210 CE) - The first [Gospel] is written according to Matthew, the same that was once a tax collector, but afterwards an apoltle of Jesus Christ who having published it for the Jewish believers, wrote it in Hebrew. [A quote by Eusebius; Eccl. Hist. 6:25]

Eusebius (315 CE) - Matthew also, having first proclaimed the Gospel in Hebrew, when on the point of going also to the other nations, committed it to writing in his native tongue, and thus supplied the want of his presence to them by his writings. [Eccl.

Hist. 3:24]

Epiphanius (370 CE) - They [The Nazarenes] have the Gospel according to Matthew quite complete in Hebrew, for this Gospel is certainly still preserved among them as it was first written, in Hebrew letters. [Panarion 29:9:4]

Jerome (382 CE) - Matthew, who is also Levi, and from a tax collectore came to be an Apostle first of all evangelists composed a Gospel of Christ in Judea in the Hebrew language and letters, for the benefit of those of the circumcision who had believed, who translated it into Greek is not sufficiently ascertained. Furthermore, the Hebrew itself is preserved to this day in the library at Caesarea, which the martyr Pamphilus so diligently collected. I also was allowed by the Nazarenes who use this volume in the Syrian cityof Borea to copy it. In which is to be remarked that, wherever the evangelist.... makes use of the testimonies of the Old Scripture, he does not follow the authority of the seventy translators, but that of the Hebrew. [Lives of Illustrious Men, Book 5]

Isho'dad (850 CE) - His [Matthew's] book was in existence in Caesarea of Palestine, and everyone acknowledges that he wrote it with his hands in Hebrew. [Isho'dad Commentary on the Gospels]

These early church quotes support the idea that Matthew wrote only to the Jews and not to the gentiles. Why is this important? If you were living in the time of Matthew and you were not a Jew who could read Hebrew then what gospel would you read in order to hear the words of Jesus? You might have to read Luke who wrote to Theophilus, a gentile. Matthew's gospel is a Jewish letter with a genre that only Jews would have understood. With that in mind let's compare all three gospels in regards to the Olivet Discourse chapters. Then we will discuss why John the apostle does not write about such an event.

Matthew 24	Mark 13	Luke 21
[1]Then Jesus went out and departed from the temple, and His disciples came up to show Him **the buildings of the temple.** [2]And Jesus said to them, "Do you not see all these things? Assuredly, I say to you, **not one stone shall be left here upon another, that shall not be thrown down."**	[1]Then as He went out of the temple, one of His disciples said to Him, "Teacher, see **what manner of stones and what buildings are here!"** [2]And Jesus answered and said to him, "Do you see these great buildings? **Not one stone shall be left upon another that shall not be thrown down."**	[5]Then, as some spoke of the temple, how it was **adorned with beautiful stones and donations,** He said, [6]"These things which you see--the days will come in which **not one stone shall be left upon another that shall not be thrown down."**

So far we see that each of the three gospels is in harmony with each other. They all agree that the Temple will be destroyed and that not one stone will be left upon another but be thrown down. Let's continue with the next verses.

Matthew 24	Mark 13	Luke 21
[3]Now as He sat on the Mount of Olives, the disciples came to Him privately, saying, "Tell us, when will these things be? **And what will be the sign of Your coming, and of the end of the age?"** [4]And Jesus answered and said to them: "Take heed that no one deceives **you. [5]For many will come in My name, saying, "I am the Christ,' and will deceive many.**[6]And you will **hear of wars** and **rumors of wars**. See that you	[3]Now as He sat on the Mount of Olives opposite the temple, Peter, James, John, and Andrew asked Him privately, [4]"Tell us, when will these things be? **And what will be the sign when all these things will be fulfilled?"** [5]And Jesus, answering them, began to say: "Take heed that no one deceives **you. [6]For many will come in My name, saying, "I am He,' and will deceive many.** [7]But when you **hear of wars**	[7]So they asked Him, saying, "Teacher, **but when will these things be? And what sign will there be when these things are about to take place?"** [8]And He said: "Take heed that **you** not be deceived. **For many will come in My name, saying, "I am He,' and, "The time has drawn near.' Therefore do not go after them.** [9]But when you **hear of wars and** commotions, do not be terrified; for these things must come to

are not troubled; for all these things must come to pass, **but the end is not yet.** [7]For nation will rise against nation, and **kingdom against kingdom**. And there will be **famines, pestilences, and earthquakes in various places.** [8]All these are the beginning of sorrows. [9]"Then they will **deliver you** up **to tribulation and kill you**, and **you** will be hated by all nations **for My name's sake.** [10]And then many will be offended, will betray one another, and will hate one another. [11]**Then many false**

and **rumors of wars,** do not be troubled; for such things must happen, **but the end is not yet.** [8]For nation will rise against nation, and **kingdom against kingdom**. And there will be **earthquakes in various places, and there will be famines and troubles**. These are the beginnings of sorrows. [9]"But watch out for yourselves, for they will **deliver you** up to councils, and you will be beaten in **the synagogues**. You will be brought before rulers and kings **for My sake,** for a testimony to

pass first, **but the end will not come** immediately." [10]Then He said to them, "Nation will rise against nation, and **kingdom against kingdom.** [11]And there will be **great earthquakes in various places, and famines and pestilences;** and there will be fearful sights and great signs from heaven. [12]But before all these things, they will lay their hands on you and persecute you, **delivering you** up to **the synagogues** and prisons. You will be brought before kings and rulers **for My name's sake.** [13]But it

prophets will rise up and deceive many. [12]And because lawlessness will abound, the love of many will grow cold. [13]**But he who endures to the end shall be saved.** [14]And this gospel of the kingdom will be preached in all the world as a witness to all the nations, and then the end will come.

them. [10]And the gospel must first be preached to all the nations. [11]But when they arrest **you** and deliver **you** up, do not worry beforehand, or premeditate what **you** will speak. But whatever is given **you** in that hour, speak that; for it is not **you** who speak, but the Holy Spirit. [12]Now brother will betray brother to death, and a father his child; and children will rise up against parents and cause them to be put to death. [13]And you will be hated by all for My name's sake. **But he who endures**

will turn out for **you** as an occasion for testimony. [14]Therefore settle it in your hearts not to meditate beforehand on what **you** will answer; [15]for I will give **you** a mouth and wisdom which all your adversaries will not be able to contradict or resist. [16]**You** will be betrayed even by parents and brothers, relatives and friends; and they will put some of **you** to death. [17]And you will be hated by all for My name's sake. [18]But not a hair of your head shall be lost. [19]**By your patience possess**

	to the end shall be saved.	your souls.

So far again we see the same message being preached about what the apostles are going to experience right before the destruction of the Temple and the exile of the Jewish people. Notice the black high lights in comparison. Matthew is the only one who talks about false prophets which fits well with his Hebrew genre. Matthew is warning against false prophets like the Old Testament prophets did back in their day. The Old Testament prophets warned Israel to repent and to stop listening to their false prophets who were speaking against God. Also notice all the *"you"* in the verses. The *"you"* are the apostles that Jesus is speaking to and giving warning too. Remember these are narratives and not letters of instruction like Paul's letters.

Matthew is also the only one who mentions the gospel of the kingdom which is related to the Jews. Let us continue with the comparison. **Note: End of the age is the Jewish age, 1Cor.10:1-11**

Matthew 24	Mark 13	Luke 21
[15]"**Therefore when you see** the "abomination of **desolation**,' spoken of by Daniel the prophet, erected in	[14]"**So when you see** the "abomination of **desolation**,' spoken of by Daniel the prophet, erected where it ought not"	[20]"**But when you see** Jerusalem surrounded by armies, then know that its **desolation** is near. [21]Then let those

the holy place" (whoever reads, let him understand), [16]"then let those who are **in Judea flee** to the mountains. [17]Let him who is on the housetop not go down to take anything out of his house. [18]And let him who is in the field not go back to get his clothes. [19]**But woe to those who are pregnant** and to those who are nursing babies in those days! [20]And pray that your flight may not be in winter or on the Sabbath. [21]For then there will be **great tribulation,** such as has not been since the beginning

(let the reader understand), "then let those who are **in Judea flee** to the mountains. [15]Let him who is on the housetop not go down into the house, nor enter to take anything out of his house. [16]And let him who is in the field not go back to get his clothes. [17]**But woe to those who are pregnant** and to those who are nursing babies in those days! [18]And pray that your flight may not be in winter. [19]For in those days there will be **tribulation**, such as has not been since the beginning of the

who are **in Judea flee** to the mountains, let those who are in the midst of her depart, and let not those who are in the country enter her. [22]For these are the days of vengeance, that all things which are written may be fulfilled. [23]**But woe to those who are pregnant** and to those who are nursing babies in those days! For there will be **great distress** in the land and **wrath upon this people**. [24]And they will fall by the edge of the sword, and be led away captive into all nations. **And Jerusalem** will be of the world until this time, no, nor ever shall be. ²²And unless those days were shortened, no flesh would be saved; but for the **elect's sake** those days will be shortened. ²³"Then if anyone says to you, "Look, here is the Christ!' or "There!' do not believe it. ²⁴For false christs and false prophets will rise and show great signs and wonders to deceive, if possible, even **the elect**. ²⁵See, I have told you beforehand. ²⁶"Therefore if they say to you, "Look, He is in the desert!' do not go out; or

creation which God created until this time, nor ever shall be. ²⁰And unless the Lord had shortened those days, no flesh would be saved; but for the **elect's sake**, whom He chose, He shortened the days. ²¹"Then if anyone says to you, "Look, here is the Christ!' or, "Look, He is there!' do not believe it. ²²For false christs and false prophets will rise and show signs and wonders to deceive, if possible, even **the elect**. ²³But take heed; see, I have told you all things beforehand.

trampled by Gentiles until the times of the Gentiles are fulfilled.

"Look, He is in the inner rooms!' do not believe it. [27]For as the lightning comes from the east and flashes to the west, so also will the coming of the Son of Man be. [28]For wherever the carcass is, there the eagles will be gathered together.		

We continue the see the same warning to Jerusalem and Israel in all three gospels. The same words being used like, *desolation, flee from Judea, pregnant, tribulation and distress.* Since Matthew's genre is Jewish in origin we must understand that his gospel will be different based on the fact that he is relating his message back to the Old Testament imagery. Jesus is not telling three different stories but one and each writing is based on the audience at hand. Mark is relating more with Matthew because Mark is using Matthews's narrative. Phrases like *"the coming of the Son of Man"* are common phrases about YHWH coming in the Old Testament and bringing judgment. For example read Isaiah 19:1 where YHWH is coming on a cloud to Egypt and is about to judge the people and it also mentions in verse 2 about brother against brother and kingdom against kingdom.

Sound familiar in the narratives we are looking at? Let us continue to compare the gospels.

Matthew 24	Mark 13	Luke 21
[29]"Immediately after the tribulation of those days **the sun will be darkened, and the moon will not give its light; the stars will fall from heaven,** and the powers of the heavens will be shaken. [30]Then the sign of the Son of Man will appear in heaven, and then all the tribes of the earth will mourn, and **they will see the Son of Man coming on the clouds of heaven with power and great glory.** [31]And He will send His	[24]"But in those days, after that tribulation, **the sun will be darkened, and the moon will not give its light;** [25]**the stars of heaven will fall,** and the powers in the heavens will be shaken. [26]**Then they will see the Son of Man coming in the clouds with great power and glory.** [27]And then He will send His angels, and gather together His elect from the four winds, from the farthest part of earth to the farthest part of heaven.	[25]"And there will be signs in **the sun, in the moon, and in the stars;** and on the earth distress of nations, with perplexity, the sea and the waves roaring; [26]men's hearts failing them from fear and the expectation of those things which are coming on the earth, for the powers of the heavens will be shaken. [27]**Then they will see the Son of Man coming in a cloud with power and great glory.** [28]Now when these

angels with a great sound of a trumpet, and they will gather together His elect from the four winds, from one end of heaven to the other.		things begin to happen, look up and lift up your heads, because your redemption draws near."

In these passages of scripture we continue to read the same events unfolding around Jerusalem. Luke is writing to a non Jew who would understand that Jerusalem and the temple are not going to be standing in the near future. The language is Jewish apocalyptic literature and it comes from the Old Testament. Matthew 13:36-43 explains the gathering of the elect as being the wicked Jews and the son of man will send out his messengers to gather them out of the kingdom. Matthew 13:36-43 reads like the above gospels regarding the elect being gathered.

Matthew 24	Mark 13	Luke 21
[32]**"Now learn this parable from the fig tree:** When its branch has already become tender and puts forth leaves, you know that summer is	[28]**"Now learn this parable from the fig tree:** When its branch has already become tender, and puts forth leaves, you know that summer is	[29]**Then He spoke to them a parable: "Look at the fig tree,** and all the trees. [30]When they are already budding, you see and know for

near. [33]So you also, when **you see** all these things, know that it is near--at the doors! [34]Assuredly, I say to you, **this generation** will by no means pass away till all these things take place. [35]Heaven and earth will pass away, but My words will by no means pass away.	near. [29]So you also, when **you see** these things happening, know that it is near--at the doors! [30]Assuredly, I say to you, **this generation** will by no means pass away till all these things take place. [31]Heaven and earth will pass away, but My words will by no means pass away.	yourselves that summer is now near. [31]So you also, when **you see** these things happening, know that the kingdom of God is near. [32]Assuredly, I say to you, **this generation** will by no means pass away till all things take place. [33]Heaven and earth will pass away, but My words will by no means pass away.

THE FIG TREE

The parable of the fig true has been the most miss understood passage and the most abused in the N.T. Almost all prophecy teachers teach that this parable is about the Jews returning back to Israel and is thee major sign that we are in the last days. The worse thing about this understanding is that the parable of the fig tree is found in Luke 13:6 and it has nothing to do with the Jews returning back to Israel. Jesus explains the parable of the fig tree as Israel's warning for 3 years and still she has not produced any fruit so she must be cut down and thrown into the fire. The fig tree in the O.T. as always represented Israel and Jesus is using the fig tree once again to represent Israel who continues to be in wickedness. Any Jewish rabbi in the 1st century would have understood this parable of the fig tree as representing the nation Israel. In all three gospels the fig tree has no fruit mentioned on the tree. This parable is not a positive one as some people would like you to believe.

THIS OR THAT GENERATION?

Finally we see that it is the generation that is standing at the time of Jesus who will not pass until all those things have been fulfilled. Nowhere does it say *"that generation"* in regards to a 2000+ years plus generation. Jesus is speaking to his apostles about the coming tribulation that is about to come on Jerusalem once again. The warnings are found in Leviticus 26:14-33. In Luke 11:37-52 we read about Jesus giving the curses to the Pharisees and telling them in verse 50 that it is *"this generation"* that will see judgment from God and they will be charged for there wickedness. There was not *"that generation"* in some future that nobody knew about. The tense is in the present not he future. Luke 11 is also found in Matthew 23 right before 24 begin.

The last thing we must look at is found in Matthew 10:16-23 where we find the same kind of language as in Matthew 24. Jesus warns the disciples of future persecution exactly as described in Matthew 24. They are told they would be handed over to the courts in the synagogues and be beaten for Jesus name sake. He goes on by saying to them that it is the one who has endured to the end who will be saved. Jesus then concludes by telling them the following:

"But when they persecute you in **this city (Jerusalem)**, *flee to another. For truly I say to you, In no way will you have finished all the cities of the House of Israel until the Son of Man will come."* **(Matthew 10:23)**

This is the most damaging passage to any believer who thinks that Matthew 24, Mark 13 and Luke 21 are about some future events with antichrist making some peace treaty and then breaking it to go stand in the temple and claim to be God. These are historical events that the gospel writers are talking about. We must maintain the historical context and the historical setting of the narrative.

THE BOOK OF REVELATION

In this part of the book I will be using Dr. Kenneth Gentry's article he wrote on, *"The Book of Revelation and Eschatology"* He has been kind enough to allow me to use this article for my books on eschatology. For a fuller, in-depth treatment of this topic see: Kenneth L. Gentry, Jr., Before Jerusalem Fell: Dating the Book of Revelation." This book is available at: KennethGentry.com.

The Book of Revelation and Eschatology
By Dr. Kenneth L. Gentry, Jr.

In this presentation I will deal with the Book of Revelation. I will particularly speak to the issues of its date of composition and theme. In that establishing Revelation's time of origin is a crucial issue for the proper interpretation of the book, I will begin with a brief presentation of the case for the early dating of Revelation. In that understanding the flow and purpose of Revelation should be among the interpreter's leading goals, I will deal a little more at length with the question of the book's theme. Once the question of *when* Revelation was written is resolved, I believe the question of *what* it is about becomes more evident.

The Date of Composition

There are two basic positions on the dating of Revelation, although each has several slight variations. The current majority position is the late-date view. This view holds that John wrote Revelation toward the close of the reign of Domitian Caesar—about A.D. 95 or 96. The minority view-point today is the early-date position. Early-date advocates hold that Revelation was written by John prior to the destruction of Jerusalem and the Temple in A.D. 70.

I hold that Revelation was produced prior to the death of Nero in June, A.D. 68, and even before the formal engagement of the Jewish War by Vespasian in spring, A.D. 67. My position is that Revelation was written in A.D. 65 or 66. This would be after the outbreak of the Neronic persecution in November, 64, and before the engagement of Vespasian's forces in spring of 67.

Though the late-date view is the majority position today, this has not always been the case. In fact, it is the opposite of what prevailed among leading biblical scholars a little over seventy-five years ago. Late-date advocate William Milligan conceded in 1893 that "recent scholarship has, with little exception, decided in favour of the earlier and not the later date." Two-decades later in 1910 early-date advocate Philip Schaff could still confirm Milligan's report: "The early date is now accepted by perhaps the majority of scholars."

In the 1800s and early 1900s the early-date position was held by such worthies as Moses Stuart, Friederich Dhsterdieck, B. F. Westcott, F. J. A. Hort, Joseph B. Lightfoot, F. W. Farrar, Alfred

Edersheim, Philip Schaff, Milton Terry, Augustus Strong, and others. Though in eclipse presently, the early-date view has not totally faded away, however. More recent advocates of the early-date include Albert A. Bell, F. F. Bruce, Rudolf Bultmann, C. C. Torrey, J. A. T. Robinson, J. A. Fitzmeyer, J. M. Ford, C. F. D. Moule, Cornelius Vanderwaal, and others.

But rather than committing an *ad verecundiam* fallacy, let us move beyond any appeal to authority to consider very briefly the argument for the early date of Revelation. Due to time constraints, I will succinctly engage only three of the internal indicators of composition date. The internal evidence should hold priority for the evangelical Christian in that it is evidence from Revelation's *self-witness*. I will only summarily allude to the arguments from *tradition* before concluding this matter. Generally it is the practice of late-date advocates to begin with the evidence from tradition, while early-date advocates start with the evidence from self-witness.

The Temple in Revelation 11

In Revelation 11:1, 2 we read:

And there was given me a reed like unto a rod: and the angel stood, saying, Rise, and measure the temple of God, and the altar, and them that worship therein. But the court which is without the temple leave out, and measure it not; for it is given unto the Gentiles: and the holy city shall they tread under foot forty and two months.

Here we find a Temple standing in a city called "the holy city."

Surely John, a Christian Jew, has in mind historical Jerusalem when he speaks of "the holy city." This seems necessary in that John is writing scripture and Jerusalem is frequently called the "holy city" in the Bible. For example: Isaiah 48:2; 52:1; Daniel 9:24; Nehemiah 11:1-18; Matthew 4:5; 27:53. In addition, verse 8 informs us that this is the city where "also our Lord was crucified." This was historical Jerusalem, according to the clear testimony of Scripture (Luke 9:22; 13:32; 17:11; 19:28). Interestingly, historical Jerusalem is never mentioned by name in Revelation. This may be due to the name "Jerusalem" meaning "city of peace." In Revelation the meanings of specific names are important to the dramatic imagery. And so it would be inappropriate to apply the name "Jerusalem" to the city upon which woe and destruction are wreaked.

Now what Temple stood in Jerusalem? Obviously the Jewish Temple ordained of God, wherein the Jewish sacrifices were offered. In the first century it was known as Herod's Temple. This reference to the Temple must be that historical structure for four reasons: It was located in Jerusalem, as the text clearly states in verse 8. This can only refer to the Herodian Temple, which appears over and over again in the New Testament record. It was the very Temple which was even the subject of one of Christ's longer prophetic discourses (Matt. 23:37-24:2ff).

Revelation 11:1, 2, written by the beloved disciple and hearer of Christ, seems clearly to draw upon Jesus' statement from the Olivet Discourse. In Luke 21:5-7, the disciples specifically point to the

Herodian Temple to inquire of its future; in Revelation 11:1 John specifically speaks of the Temple of God. In Luke 21:6 Jesus tells His disciples that the Temple will soon be destroyed stone by stone. A comparison of Luke 21:24 and Revelation 11:2 strongly suggests that the source of Revelation's statement is Christ's word in Luke 21. [Luke 21:24b: "Jerusalem will be *trampled underfoot* by the *Gentiles* until the *times of the Gentiles be fulfilled.*" Revelation 11:2b: "it is given unto the *Gentiles*: and the *holy city* shall they *tread under foot* for *forty and two months*." The two passages speak of the same unique event and even employ virtually identical terms. According to Revelation 11:2 Jerusalem and the Temple were to be under assault for a period of forty-two months. We know from history that the Jewish War with Rome was formally engaged in Spring, A.D. 67, and was won with the collapse of the Temple in August, A.D. 70. This is a period of forty-two months, which fits the precise measurement of John's prophecy. John's prophecy antedates the outbreak of the Jewish War.

After the reference to the destruction of the "temple of God" in the "holy city," John later speaks of a "new Jerusalem" coming down out of heaven, which is called the "holy city" (Rev. 21:2) and which does not need a temple (Rev. 21:22). This *new* Jerusalem is apparently meant to supplant the old Jerusalem with its temple system. The old order Temple was destroyed in August, A.D. 70.

Thus, while John wrote, the Temple was still standing, awaiting its approaching doom. If John wrote this twenty-five years *after* the

Temple's fall it would be terribly anachronous. The reference to the Temple is hard architectural evidence that gets us back into an era pre-A.D. 70.

The Seven Kings in Revelation 17

In Revelation 17:1-6 a vision of a seven-headed beast is recorded. In this vision we discover strong evidence that Revelation was written *before* the death of Nero, which occurred on June 8, A.D. 68. John wrote to be understood. The first of seven benedictions occurs in his introduction: "Blessed is he that reads, and they that hear the words of this prophecy, and keep those things which are written therein" (Rev. 1:3). And just after the vision itself is given in Revelation 17:1-6, an interpretive angel appears for the express purpose of *explaining* the vision: "And the angel said unto me, Wherefore didst thou marvel? I will tell thee the mystery of the woman, and of the beast that carrieth her, which hath the seven heads and ten horns" (Rev 17:7). Then in verses 9 and 10 this angel explains the vision: "Here is the mind which hath wisdom. The seven heads are seven mountains, on which the woman sitteth. And there are seven kings: five are fallen, and one is, and the other is not yet come; and when he cometh, he must continue a short space." Most evangelical scholars recognize that the seven mountains represent the famed Seven Hills of Rome. The recipients of Revelation lived under the rule of Rome, which was universally distinguished by its seven hills. How could the recipients, living in the seven historical churches of Asia Minor and under Roman imperial rule, understand anything else but this geographical feature?

But there is an additional difficulty involved. The seven heads have a *two-fold* referent. We learn also that the seven heads represent a *political* situation in which five kings have fallen, the sixth is, and the seventh is yet to come and will remain but a short while. It is surely no accident that Nero was the sixth emperor of Rome, who reigned after the deaths of his five predecessors and before the brief rule of the seventh emperor.

Flavius Josephus, the Jewish contemporary of John, clearly points out that Julius Caesar was the first emperor of Rome and that he was followed in succession by Augustus, Tiberius, Caius, Claudius, and Nero (*Antiquities* 18; 19). We discover this enumeration also in other near contemporaries of John: 4 Ezra 11 and 12; Sibylline Oracles, books 5 and 8; Barnabas, *Epistle* 4; Suetonius, *Lives of the Twelve Caesars*; and Dio Cassius' *Roman History* 5.

The text of Revelation says of the seven kings "five have fallen." The first five emperors are dead, when John writes. But the verse goes on to say "one is." That is, the sixth one is *then reigning* even as John wrote. That would be Nero Caesar, who assumed imperial power upon the death of Claudius in October, A.D. 54, and remained emperor until June, A.D. 68.

John continues: "The other is not yet come; and when he comes, he must continue a short space." When the Roman Civil Wars broke out in rebellion against him, Nero committed suicide on June 8, A.D. 68. The seventh king was "not yet come." That would be Galba, who assumed power in June, A.D. 68. But he was only to continue a "short space." His reign lasted but six months, until January 15, A.D. 69.

Thus, we see that while John wrote, Nero was still alive and Galba was looming in the near future. Revelation could not have been written after June, A.D. 68, according to the internal political evidence.

The Jews in Revelation

The final evidence from Revelation's self-witness that I will consider is the relationship of the Jew to Christianity in Revelation. And although there are several aspects of this evidence, we will just briefly introduce it. Two important passages and their implications may be referred to illustratively.

First, when John writes Revelation, Christians are tensely mingled with the Jews. Christianity is deemed the true Israel and Christians the real Jews. In Revelation 2:9 we read of Jesus' word to one of His churches of the day: "I know your tribulation and your poverty (but you are rich), and the blasphemy by those who say they are Jews and are not, but are a synagogue of Satan."

Who but a Jew would call himself a Jew? But in the early formative history of Christianity, believers are everywhere in the New Testament presented as "Abraham's seed," "the circumcision," "the Israel of God," the "true Jew," etc.

We must remember that even Paul, the apostle to the Gentiles, took

Jewish vows and had Timothy circumcised. But after the destruction of the Temple (A.D. 70) there was no tendency to inter-mingling. In fact, the famed Jewish rabbi, Gamaliel II, put a curse on Christians in the daily benediction, which virtually forbad social inter-mingling. In Revelation the Jews are represented as emptily calling themselves "Jews." They are not true Jews in the fundamental, spiritual sense, which was Paul's argument in Romans 2. This would suggest a date prior to the final separation of Judaism and Christianity. Christianity was a protected religion under Rome's *religio licita* legislation, *as long as it was considered a sect of Judaism*. The legal separation of Christianity from Judaism was in its earliest stages, beginning with the Neronic persecution in late A.D. 64. It was finalized both legally and culturally with the Temple's destruction, as virtually all historical and New Testament scholars agree. Interestingly, in the A.D. 80s the Christian writer Barnabas makes a radical "us/them" division between Israel and the Church (*Epistle* 13:1).

Second, at the time John writes, things are in the initial stages of a fundamental change. Revelation 3:9 reads: "Behold, I will cause those of the synagogue of Satan, who say that they are Jews, and are not, but lie -- behold, I will make them to come and bow down at your feet, and to know that I have loved you."
John points to the approaching humiliation of the Jews, noting that God will vindicate His Church against them. In effect, He would make the Jews to lie down at the Christian's feet. This can have reference to nothing other than the destruction of Israel and the Temple, which was prophesied by Christ. After that horrible event

Christians began making reference to the Temple's destruction as an apologetic and vindication of Christianity. Ignatius (A.D. 107) is a classic example of this in his *Magnesians* 10. There are scores of such references in such writers as Melito, Tertullian, Clement of Alexandria, Lactantius, and others.

There are other arguments regarding the Jewish character of Revelation, such as its grammar, its reference to the twelve tribes, allusions to the priestly system, temple worship, and so forth. The point seems clear enough: When John writes Revelation, Christianity is not divorced from Israel. After A.D. 70 such would not be the case. This is strong socio-cultural evidence for a pre-A.D. 70 composition.

Conclusion

I have surveyed the political evidence regarding the Seven Kings, the architectural evidence of the standing Temple, and the socio- cultural evidence of the uneasy Jew/Christian mixture. These suggest Revelation was written prior to the destruction of the Temple in August, 70, and even before the death of Nero Caesar, which occurred on June 8, 68. I believe we can even press it back before the formal engagement of the Jewish War in 67, though not before the outbreak of the Neronic persecution beginning in November, 64.

Were time available we could consider the external evidence. I believe a case may be made for the reconstruction of Irenaeus' famous statement, which is *the* major evidence form tradition. This would allow for an early-date for Revelation by applying his reference about the reign of Domitian to *John himself* regarding his *active ministry*, rather than to John's *writing of Revelation*.

With a great number of biblical scholars, I am convinced that the Shepherd of Hermas shows dependence on Revelation. I also believe there is evidence for the Shepherd's date of writing in the late 80s. The Muratorian Canon says John wrote letters to seven churches *before* Paul finished his church letters, which were to seven different congregations. Tertullian relates a tradition that seems to indicate John was banished at about the same time as Peter and Paul were martyred. Clement of Alexandria informs us that all revelation ceased under Nero's reign. He makes this claim while elsewhere holding that John's Revelation was inspired of God. Epiphanius dates Revelation under Claudius' reign. This is either a wild, unaccountable, and unique error, or it is a reference to Nero by his other name. Nero's full adoptive name was Nero Claudius Caesar. Various Syriac manuscripts specifically assign John's banishment to the reign of Nero. Arethas interprets many of the prophecies of Revelation as being fulfilled in the Jewish War and Andreas has to combat such interpretations in his day.

I believe the early-date of Revelation may be firmly established in the seventh decade of the first century, not the last. Having come to this conclusion; let me now turn to consider:

The Theme of Revelation

When interpreting any book of the Bible, it is important for us to understand the audience to which it was originally directed. There are at least three factors in Revelation that emphasize the original audience and their historic circumstances. These *begin* to move us toward the preterist position. When these are combined with the matter of the *expectation* of Revelation (with which I will deal in a moment), the preterist approach becomes justified on the basis of sound hermeneutical principle.

Audience Relevance

First, in Revelation we have clear evidence that John is writing to particular, historic, individual churches that existed in his day. Revelation 1:4a reads: "John to the seven churches which are in Asia." In verse 11 he specifically names the seven churches to whom he speaks. We know these are historical cities containing historical churches. These churches are specifically dealt with in terms of their historically and culturally unique circumstances in chapters 2 and 3. Real first century Christians are being addressed.

Second, as I indicated previously, John writes to these churches in order to be *understood*. Revelation 1:3 reads: "Blessed [is] he that readeth, and they that hear the words of this prophecy, and keep those things which are written therein." Real first century Christians are expected to understand and to heed John's message as something most relevant to them.

Third, in Revelation John notes that he and the seven churches have *already* entered "the tribulation" (Rev. 1:9a): "I John, who also am your brother, and companion in the tribulation, and in the kingdom and patience of Jesus Christ, was in the isle that is called Patmos, for the word of God, and for the testimony of Jesus Christ." In Revelation 2 and 3 there are allusions to greater problems brewing on the world scene. Real first century Christians were to have a deep and personal concern with the era in which they lived.

Contemporary Expectation

It is terribly important that the interpreter of Revelation begin at the first verses of the book and let them lead him to the proper interpretive approach. The truth of the matter is: *John specifically states that the prophecies of Revelation, which were written to seven historical churches, would begin coming to pass within a very short period of time*. He emphasized this truth in a variety of ways. Let us briefly note his contemporary expectation from two angles.

First, we should note that he *varies his manner of expression*, as if to avoid any potential confusion as to his meaning. The first of these terms we come upon in Revelation is the Greek word *tachos*, translated "shortly." John is explaining the purpose of his writing in Revelation 1:1, which reads: "The Revelation of Jesus Christ, which God gave Him to show to His bond-servants, the things which must *shortly* [*tachos*] take place." This term also occurs in Revelation 2:16; 3:11; and 22:6, 7, 12, 20.

Another term John uses is *eggus*, which means "near." This term is found in Revelation 1:3 and 22:10. In Revelation 1:3 we read:

"Blessed is he who reads and those who hear the words of the prophecy, and heeds the things which are written in it; for the time is *near* (*eggus*)." Revelation 22:10 reads: "And he saith unto me, 'Seal not the sayings of the prophecy of this book: for the time is *at hand* (*eggus*).'" The import of *eggus* in our context is clearly that of *temporal* nearness.

Second, John emphasizes his anticipation of the soon occurrence of his prophecy by *strategic placement* of these time references. He places his boldest time statements in both the introduction and conclusion to Revelation. The statement of expectancy is found twice in the first three verses: Revelation 1:1 and 3. The same idea is found four times in his concluding remarks: Revelation 22:6, 7, 12, 20. *It is as if John carefully bracketed the entire work to avoid any confusion.* It is important to note that these statements occur in the more historical and didactic sections of Revelation, before and after the major dramatic-symbolic visions.

With the particularity of the audience emphasized in conjunction with his message of the imminent expectation of the occurrence of the events, I do not see how a preterism of some sort can be escaped.

Theme Statement
The theme of Revelation is found in Revelation 1:7: "Behold, He is coming with the clouds, and every eye will see Him, even those who pierced Him; and all the tribes of the earth will mourn over Him. Even so. Amen."

I am convinced that the apocalyptic language in this passage must be applied to Christ's *judgment-coming upon Israel*, rather than to the Second Advent at the end of temporal history. The events of A.D. 70, like those associated with the collapse of Babylon, Egypt, and other nations, are typological foreshadowings of the consummational Second Advent.

Cloud-comings are frequent prophetic emblems in the Old Testament. They serve as indicators of divine visitations of judgment upon ancient, historical nations. God "comes" in *judicial judgment* upon Israel's enemies in general (Psa. 18:7-15; 104:3), upon Egypt (Isa. 19:1), upon disobedient Israel in the Old Testament (Joel 2:1,2), and so forth. To cite one example, Isaiah 19:1 says: "Behold, the LORD rideth upon a swift cloud, and shall come into Egypt: and the idols of Egypt shall be moved at his presence, and the heart of Egypt shall melt in the midst of it."

A coming of Christ in judgment upon Israel is clearly taught in parabolic form by Christ in Matthew 21:40, 41, 43, 45:
When the lord therefore of the vineyard cometh, what will he do unto those husbandmen? They say unto him, He will miserably destroy those wicked men, and will let out [his] vineyard unto other husbandmen, which shall render him the fruits in their seasons.... Therefore say I unto you, The kingdom of God shall be taken from you, and given to a nation bringing forth the fruits thereof.... And when the chief priests and Pharisees had heard his parables, they perceived that he spake of them.

This surely speaks of the destruction of the Jerusalem of the chief priests and Pharisees of Jesus' day. And it will occur "when the Lord of the vineyard comes." This is the judgment-coming of Christ in A.D. 70.

For several reasons I am convinced that Revelation 1:7 also refers to His coming in judgment upon Israel.

First, this coming is a judgment-coming upon "those who pierced Him." The New Testament emphatically points to first century Israel as responsible for crucifying Christ. Israel forced the hand of the Roman procurator, Pontius Pilate, when the Jews cried out in John 19:15: "'Away with him, away with him, crucify him.' Pilate saith unto them, 'Shall I crucify your King?' The chief priests answered, 'We have no king but Caesar.'" See also: Acts 2:22-23, 36; 3:13-15; 5:30; 7:52; 1 Thess. 2:14-15.

Second, Revelation 1:7 states that as a consequence of this judgment "all the tribes (*phule*) of the Land (*he ge*) will mourn." "The Land" is a familiar designation for Israel's Promised Land. And as is well known, Israel was divided into twelve tribes. In fact, Revelation 7 has the marking out of 144,000 from among the specifically designated twelve tribes of Israel before the winds of destruction blow upon the "land." When Revelation broadens the definition of "tribes" to incorporate non-Jews, it does not speak of "the land" (*he ge*), but "the nations" (*ethnoi*).

Third, Jesus even told the first century Jewish leaders that they would witness this judgment-coming. In Matthew 26:63-64 we read: "But Jesus held his peace. And the high priest answered and said unto him, 'I adjure thee by the living God, that thou tell us whether thou be the Christ, the Son of God.' Jesus saith unto him, 'Thou hast said: nevertheless I say unto you, Hereafter shall ye see the Son of man sitting on the right hand of power, and coming in the clouds of heaven.'"

This coming, dealt with at length in Matthew 24:1-34 was to occur in His generation. Matthew 24:30 and 34 read: "And then shall appear the sign of the Son of man in heaven: and then shall all the tribes of the earth mourn, and they shall see the Son of man coming in the clouds of heaven with power and great glory.... Verily I say unto you, this generation shall not pass, till all these things be fulfilled."

Drawing this information together, along with the historical facts of the era, we learn that:

 The Jewish War with Rome from 67 to 70 brought about the deaths of tens of thousands of the Jews in Judea, and the enslavement of thousands upon thousands more. The Jewish historian Flavius Josephus, who was an eye-witness, records that 1.1 million Jews perished in the siege of Jerusalem.

But as awful as the Jewish loss of life was, the utter devastation of

Jerusalem, the final destruction of the temple, and the conclusive cessation of the sacrificial system were lamented even more. The covenantal significance of the loss of the temple stands as the most dramatic outcome of the War. It was an unrepeatable loss, for the temple has never been rebuilt. The old covenant era was forever closed. Hence, any Jewish calamity after A.D. 70 would pale in comparison to the redemptive-historical significance of the loss of the temple.

Thematic Character

Before we can actually develop the flow of Revelation, we need to ascertain the identity of a major character in the drama presented: Who is the harlot identified in Revelation 17?

So he carried me away in the Spirit into the wilderness. And I saw a woman sitting on a scarlet beast which was full of names of blasphemy, having seven heads and ten horns.... And on her forehead a name was written: MYSTERY, BABYLON THE GREAT, THE MOTHER OF HARLOTS AND OF THE ABOMINATIONS OF THE EARTH (Rev. 17:3, 5).

Some have thought that the harlot is representative of the city of Rome because she is here seen resting upon the seven hills and she is called "Babylon." But since the Beast itself is representative of Rome, it would seem redundant to have the woman representing the same. Neither does the name "Babylon" historically belong to either Rome or Jerusalem, and thus cannot be proof that the city is Rome rather than Jerusalem. I am convinced beyond any doubt that this harlot is *Jerusalem.*

First, in Revelation 14:8 "Babylon" is called "the great city." The first mention of "the great city" in Revelation 11:8, indisputably points to Jerusalem. There we read that it is the place "where also our Lord was crucified" (cp. Luke 9:31; 13:33-34; 18:31; 24:18-20). Her greatness is in regard to her covenantal status in the Old Testament. "Jerusalem" appears in Scripture 623 times. She is called "the city of the great king" (Psa. 48:2; Matt. 5:35), "the city of God" (Psa. 46:4; 48:1; 87:3), "the joy of the whole earth" (Psa. 48:2; Lam. 2:15), and other such laudable names. She is even called "the great city" elsewhere in Scripture: "People from many nations will pass by this city and will ask one another, 'Why has the LORD done such a thing to this great city?'" (Jer. 22:8). "How deserted lies the city, once so full of people! How like a widow is she, who once was *great among the nations*! She who was queen among the provinces has now become a slave" (Lam. 1:1).

Even pagan writers speak highly of Jerusalem. Tacitus calls it "a famous city" (*Histories* 5:2). Pliny the Elder writes that Jerusalem was "by far the most famous city of the ancient Orient" (*Natural History* 5:14:70). Appian, a Roman lawyer and writer (*ca.* A.D. 160), calls her "the great city Jerusalem" (*The Syrian Wars* 50).

Second, the Babylonian harlot is filled with the blood of the saints, according to Revelation 16:6; 17:6; 18:21, 24. For instance, Revelation 18:24 reads: "And in her was found the blood of prophets and saints, and of all who were slain on the earth." Of course, with the outbreak of the Neronic persecution, which had just gotten under way, Rome was stained with the blood of the saints. Yet Rome had only recently entered the persecuting ranks of God's enemies. Throughout Acts *Jerusalem* is portrayed as the persecutor and Rome as the protector of Christianity. Furthermore, Rome was not guilty of killing any of the Old Testament prophets, as was Jerusalem. Before his stoning, Stephen rebukes Jerusalem: "Which of the *prophets* have not *your fathers persecuted*? And they have slain them who showed before of the coming of the Just One, of whom ye have been now the betrayers and murderers" (Acts 7:51-52).

In the context of the Olivet Discourse Jesus reproaches Jerusalem. Matthew 23:34-35 reads: "Therefore, indeed, I send you prophets, wise men, and scribes: some of them you will kill and crucify, and some of them you will scourge in your synagogues and persecute from city to city, that on you may come all the righteous blood shed on the earth, from the blood of righteous Abel to the blood of Zechariah, son of Berechiah, whom you murdered between the temple and the altar."

Throughout Revelation it is the *slain Lamb* who acts in judgment upon His slayers, the Jews. "Then I saw a Lamb, looking as if it had been slain, standing in the center of the throne, encircled by the four living creatures and the elders. He had seven horns and seven eyes, which are the seven spirits of God sent out into all the earth" (Rev. 5:6; cp. 5:12; 13:8). This Lamb is mentioned twenty-seven times in

Revelation. And Jerusalem literally called down judgment upon herself for slaying the Lamb of God: "All the people answered, 'Let his blood be on us and on our children!'" (Matt. 27:25).

Third, the harlot is arrayed in the Jewish priestly colors of scarlet, purple, and gold described in Exo. 28. These colors were also found in the Temple: Josephus carefully describes Jerusalem's Temple tapestry as "*Babylonian* tapestry in which blue, purple, scarlet and linen were mingled" (*Wars* 5:5:4). He does so while giving the color decor of the Temple much emphasis and elaboration.

The harlot even has a blasphemous inscription on her forehead that gives a negative portrayal of the holy inscription which the Jewish high priest wore. On the high priest's forehead we read: "Holy to the Lord" (Exo. 28:36-38). On the harlot's forehead we read: "Mystery, Babylon the Great, the Mother of Harlots and of the Abominations of the Earth" (Rev. 17:5). And she has a gold cup in her hand, as did the high priest on the Day of Atonement, according to the Jewish Talmud. Interestingly, the Temple's main door had on it golden vines with great clusters of grapes (from which wine is derived). The golden grape clusters on the vine were very prominent, being the size of a man (Josephus, *Wars* 5:5:4). These are suggestive of the golden cup to be filled with blood.

Fourth, there is an obvious literary contrast between the harlot and the chaste bride. This juxtaposition suggests an intentional contrast between the Jerusalem below (Rev. 11:8) and the Jerusalem above

(Rev. 21:2). This is not unfamiliar to writers of Scripture (cp. Gal. 4:24ff.; Heb. 12:18ff.). When you compare Revelation 17:2-5 and Revelation 21:1ff the contrast provides a remarkable negative and positive image. And we must remember that the bride is specifically called the "New Jerusalem" from heaven (Rev. 21:1-2). Consider: John is introduced to the *harlot* and to the *bride* in a similar fashion:

Revelation 17:1: "And there came one of the seven angels which had the seven vials, and talked with me, saying unto me, 'Come hither; I will shew unto thee the judgment of the great whore that sitteth upon many waters.'"

Revelation 21:9: "And there came unto me one of the seven angels which had the seven vials full of the seven last plagues, and talked with me, saying, 'Come hither, I will shew thee the bride, the Lamb's wife.'"

The two women are contrasted as to character.

Revelation 17:1: "Come here, I will shew unto thee the judgment of the great whore that sitteth upon many waters."

Revelation 21:9: "Come hither, I will shew thee the bride, the Lamb's wife."

The two women are seen in contrasting environments to which John is carried by the angel.

Revelation 17:3: "So he carried me away in the spirit into the wilderness and I saw a woman sit upon a scarlet coloured beast."

Revelation 21:10: "And he carried me away in the spirit to a great and high mountain, and shewed me that great city, the holy Jerusalem, descending out of heaven from God."

The dress of each is detailed and contrasted:

Revelation 17:4: "And the woman was arrayed in purple and scarlet colour, and decked with gold and precious stones and pearls, having a golden cup in her hand full of abominations and filthiness of her fornication."

Revelation 19:8; 21:11: "And to her was granted that she should be arrayed in fine linen, clean and white: for the fine linen is the righteousness of saints.... Having the glory of God: and her light [was] like unto a stone most precious, even like a jasper stone, clear as crystal."

Fifth, Jerusalem had previously been called by pagan names quite compatible with the designation "Babylon." In Revelation 11:8 she was called "spiritually Sodom and Egypt." Isaiah did the same to her in Isaiah 1 where he called Jerusalem "Sodom and Gomorrah." The idea is that rather than conducting herself as the wife of God, she had become one of His enemies like Sodom, Egypt, and Babylon. The fact that the harlot is seated on the seven-headed Beast (obviously representative of Rome) indicates not *identity* with Rome, but *alliance* with Rome against Christianity. The Jews demanded Christ's crucifixion and constantly agitated against the Christians to get the Romans involved in their persecution (cp. Matt. 23:37ff.; John 19:16-16; Acts 17:7). (I have not completed my research yet, but I believe her being seated on the beast in a drunken state represents the female-superior position in sexual intercourse. She is a drunken harlot taking the lead in her immorality. In the drama of Revelation she is not engaged in just adultery, but in bestiality, as well.

Thematic Flow

Now we are ready briefly to sketch the thematic idea of Revelation. Not only is Israel's destruction the focus of Revelation, but her judgment is set forth in an interesting and significant covenantal fashion.

Israel as the Wife of God. We must remember that in the Old Testament Israel was graciously taken by God to be His covenantal wife. Oftentimes the prophets mention the covenantal marriage relation between God and Israel.

Jeremiah 3:14: "Turn, O backsliding children, saith the LORD; for I am married unto you."
Ezekiel 16 portrays in beautiful poetic imagery, the husbandly love of God for Israel.

Ezekiel 16:8: "Now when I passed by thee, and looked upon thee, behold, thy time was the time of love; and I spread my skirt over thee, and covered thy nakedness: yea, I sware unto thee, and entered into a covenant with thee, saith the Lord GOD, and thou becamest mine."

Other passages alluding to the marriage covenant between God and Israel include: Isaiah 50:1; 54:5; 62:4; Jeremiah 3:20; 31:32; and Ezekiel 16:31-32.

As a covenantal action, Israel's marriage was formally established with proper witnesses. Deuteronomy 31:28 reads: "Gather unto me all the elders of your tribes, and your officers, that I may speak these words in their ears, and call heaven and earth to record against them." See also: Deuteronomy 4:26; 30:19.

But as an unfaithful wife Israel chased after foreign gods, committing spiritual adultery against the Lord. This adulterous infidelity is portrayed in many Old Testament passages. The old covenant prophets served as God's lawyers. As VanGemeren expresses it: "The prophets had spoken as God's covenant prosecutors, bringing God's charge and stating God's verdict." On the basis of God's Law and before witnesses, they legally called upon her to return to her covenantal husband, the Lord God. They often brought a "case" (Heb.: *ribh*) against Israel, calling heaven and earth as witnesses in this heavenly court-room drama and as per the public confirmation of the covenant.

Isaiah 1:2: "Hear, O heavens, and give ear, O earth: for the LORD hath spoken, I have nourished and brought up children, and they have rebelled against me." Isaiah laments: "How is the faithful city become an harlot!" (Isa. 1:21a).

Hosea 4:1: "Hear the word of the LORD, ye children of Israel: for the LORD hath a *controversy* with the inhabitants of the land, because there is no truth, nor mercy, nor knowledge of God in the land."

Micah 6:2: "Hear ye, O mountains, the LORD'S *controversy*, and ye strong foundations of the earth: for the LORD hath a controversy with his people, and he will plead with Israel." See also: Hos. 12:2 Ultimately, their work was futile in that Israel finally demanded the crucifixion of the Son of God, crying out: "We have no king but Caesar!"

The Divorce Decree Against Israel

The dramatic visions of Revelation are framed in such a way as to represent God's judicial divorce decree against Israel. Following upon that we witness her capital punishment for all sorts of sins, which flowed from her spiritual adultery.

In Revelation 4 God is seen seated on His judicial throne. Interestingly, God's throne is mentioned in eighteen of Revelation's twenty-two chapters. In fact, of the sixty-two appearances of the word "throne" in the New Testament, forty-seven of these are found in Revelation. The judicial element is strong in this book, including references to judgments, witnesses, and the like.

In Revelation 5 a seven sealed scroll is seen in God's hand, while He is seated upon His throne of justice. The seven sealed scroll seems to represent God's "bill of divorcement" handed down by the Judge on the throne against Israel. It is known that divorce decrees were written out among the Jews in the biblical era: Deuteronomy 24:1, 3; Isaiah 50:1; Jeremiah 3:8; Matthew 5:31; 19:7; and Mark 10:4. It is equally certain that marriage was understood in terms of a covenant contract: Proverbs 2:17; Ezekiel 16:8; and Malachi 2:14. That the scroll in Revelation 5-8 would be a bill of divorcement is suggested on the following considerations.

First, in Revelation we have prominent emphases on two particular women, two women that obviously correspond as opposites to one another. The two women are the wicked harlot of the Beast (Rev. 17-18) and the pure bride of Christ (Rev. 21). As I have shown, they correspond with the earthly Jerusalem that was the scene of Christ's crucifixion (Rev. 11:8) and the heavenly Jerusalem which is holy (Rev. 21:10). The flow and drift of the book is the revelation and execution of the legal judgment (Rev. 15:3; 16:5-7) on the fornicating harlot.

Following this we witness the coming of a virginal bride (Rev. 21), obviously to take her place after a marriage supper (Rev. 19). This fits well with the Pauline imagery in Galatians 4:24ff, where he speaks of the casting out of the one wife (Hagar who is representative of the Jerusalem below) and the taking of the other wife (Sara who is representative of the Jerusalem above).

Second, the apparent Old Testament background for this imagery is found in Ezekiel and Leviticus. In Ezekiel 2:9-10 Israel's judgment is portrayed as written on a scroll on the front and back and given to Ezekiel. This corresponds perfectly with the scroll in Revelation 5:1. In Ezekiel 2ff the devastation of Israel is outlined, which corresponds with Revelation 6ff. In Ezekiel 16 Israel is viewed as God's covenant wife which became a harlot that trusted in her beauty and committed fornication (Eze. 16:15). This is the case with Jerusalem-Babylon in Revelation (Rev. 18:7). She is cast out and judged for this evil conduct.

The reason for *seven* seals is found in covenantal imagery, as well. The seven seals on Revelation's scroll reflect the seven-fold covenantal judgment God forewarned Israel about in Leviticus 26:14-33. These judgments are threatened against *Israel,* if she should forsake God. The seven-fold judgments in Leviticus have a strong influence on the judgment language of Revelation. When these seals are opened, the preliminary judgments begin.

Third, following the "divorce" and judgments associated with it, John turns to see the coming of a new "bride" out of heaven (Rev. 21-22). It would seem that the new bride could not be taken until the harlotrous wife should first be taken care of legally. John imports the imagery of the harlot, bride, and marriage feast; this is not being read into the text from outside. Thus, the imagery of divorce well fits the dramatic flow of the work.

The Execution of the Judgments

The punishment in God's Law for adultery is death (Lev. 20:10), which in biblical law was by stoning. So we discover huge hailstones raining down on Jerusalem in Revelation 16:21: "And there fell upon men a great hail out of heaven, every stone about the weight of a talent: and men blasphemed God because of the plague of the hail; for the plague thereof was exceeding great." This was accomplished historically by the tenth legion of the Roman armies:

The engines [i.e., catapults], that all the legions had ready prepared for them, were admirably contrived; but still more extraordinary ones belonged to the tenth legion: those that threw darts and those that threw stones, were more forcible and larger than the rest, by which they not only repelled the excursions of the Jews, but drove those away that were upon the walls also. Now, the stones that were cast, were of the weight of a talent, and were carried two furlongs and further. The blow they gave was no way to be sustained, not only by those that stood first in the way, but by those that were beyond them for a great space. As for the Jews, they at first watched the coming of the stone, for it was a white colour. (*Wars* 5:6:3)

Now Israel is not only Jehovah's wife in the Old Testament, but she is to serve Him as a kingdom of priests ministering to the nations.

Thus, she is represented in Revelation as being a *harlot* in *priestly garments*. Being such, another Old Testament Law comes to bear. Leviticus 21:9 warns, "The daughter of any priest, if she profane herself by playing the harlot, she profaneth her father, she shall be burned with fire." Consequently, we see reference to Israel's being burned with fire in Revelation 17:16: "And the ten horns which thou sawest upon the beast, these shall hate the whore, and shall make her desolate and naked, and shall eat her flesh, and burn her with fire."

Then, having legally disposed of Israel as an harlotrous, priestly wife, Revelation turns to consider a new bride. In Revelation 21 we see a city coming down out of heaven adorned as a spotless virgin bride for her husband. This new city is a New Jerusalem. This "New Jerusalem" is the Church, according to Galatians 4:21ff. and Hebrews 12:18ff.

Thus, the theme of Revelation is the execution of God's divorce decree against Israel, her subsequent capital punishment and cremation, followed by His turning to take a new bride, the Church.

Conclusion

In conclusion, I believe that Revelation was written in about A.D. 65. I further believe that it speaks to the original Christian audience regarding difficulties they were facing and in explanation of the coming final removal of Jerusalem by God's wrath.

The book is to be understood preteristically, rather than

futuristically. We learn this not only from the imminent expectation in the book, but also from its theme (which involves the judgment of the Jews) and due to its leading characters: Jerusalem (as a harlot) and Rome (as a Beast).

Bibliography and References

William Milligan, *Discussions on the Apocalypse* (London: Macmillan, 1893), p. 75.

Philip Schaff, *History of the Christian Church* (3rd ed: (Grand Rapids: Eerdmans, 1950 [1910]), 1:834.

See for example: Acts 4:3; 5:18-33; 6:12; 7:54-60; 8:1ff; 9:1-4, 13, 23; 11:19; 12:1-3; 13:45-50; 14:2-5, 19; 16:23; 17:5-13; 18:12; 20:3, 19; 21:11, 27; 22:30; 23:12, 20, 27, 30; 24:5-9; 25:2-15; 25:24; 26:21. See also: 2 Cor. 11:24; 2 Thess. 2:14-15; Heb. 10:32-34; Rev. 2:9; 3:9; etc.

Jer. 2:30; Matt. 5:12; 23:34, 35; Acts 7:52; 1 Thess. 2:15.
See: Rev. 5:6, 8, 12-13; 6:1, 16; 7:9-10, 14, 17; 12:11; 13:8, 11; 14:1, 4, 10; 15:3; 17:14; 19:7, 9; 21:14, 22-23; 22:1, 3.
Cp. Rev. 17:4-5 with Exo. 25:2, 4; 26:1, 31, 36; 27:16; 28:1-2, 5-12, 15, 17-23, 33.

Golden bowls were used elsewhere in the Levitical services. See: Exo. 25:29; 37:16, 17.

See: Isaiah 1:21; 50:1; 57:8; Jeremiah 2:2, 20; 3:1-20; 4:30; 11:15; 13:27; Ezekiel 6:9; 16:32; Hosea 1:2; 2:5, 7; 3:3; 4:15; Malachi 2:7.

Willem VanGemeren, *The Progress of Redemption: The Story of Salvation from Creation to the New Jerusalem* (Grand Rapids: Zondervan, 1988), p. 290.

THE MELLENNIUM

For years we have heard about a coming millennium where Jesus will establish his kingdom on earth for a thousand years. Then after the thousand years are completed there will be a final judgment by God after Satan has been released to cause war on the earth again. Where does such a teaching come from and did the early church believe such a thing? There is only one place in the entire Bible where this thousand year teaching can be found. In Revelation 20 we read the following:

(Rev 20:4) *"And I saw thrones, and they sat on them. And judgment was given to them, and the souls of the ones having been beheaded because of the witness of Yahshua, and because of the Word of YAHWEH, and who had not worshiped the beast nor its image, and had not received the mark on their forehead and on their hand. And they lived and reigned with Messiah a thousand years.*

(Rev 20:5) *This is the first resurrection."* **(Hebraic Roots Bible)**

The firs thing we must understand is that nowhere in chapter 20 will you read anything about a kingdom being established on earth. In fact the whole vision that John is describing here is what he saw taking place in heaven after the death of the believers. In fact in verse 6 we read the following:

(Rev 20:6) *"Blessed and holy is the one having part in the first resurrection. The second death has no authority over these, but they will be priests of YAHWEH and of His Messiah, and will reign with Him a thousand years."* **(Hebraic Roots Bible)**

This passage tells us that the believers who were killed for the sake of the faith in Jesus will reign with him in heaven for a thousand years in haven and not on earth. But what does a thousand years really mean?

THE ONE THOUSAND

As for the time period of a thousand years, the Greek term used is chilioi, which is the plural of chilias. However, this is a case where we cannot simply use Strong's Concordance to prove the point. One must also know how Greek grammar works. The term "thousand years" consists of an adjective ("thousand") and a noun ("years") which it is describing. Since the noun "years" is plural, Greek grammar demands that the adjective "thousand" must also be plural. This is different from English grammar, but we cannot judge Greek grammar by English rules. And so, while we might be tempted to read the literal Greek as "thousands (of) years", in reality it should be read in English as "a thousand years."

We run across the same problem in 2 Peter 3:8. (Here Peter refers to

Psalm 90:4.) 8 . . . One day is with the Lord as a thousand (chilioi, "thousands") years, and a thousand (chilioi, "thousands") years as one day.

Once again, in Greek, the adjective must agree with the noun that it describes. In this case, "thousand" must agree with the word "years", which is plural. And so, while the literal Greek would read "thousands years", in English we must render it a "thousand years" in order to allow our translation to conform to the rules of English grammar.

By contrast, we should show an example where the word "thousand" is singular in the original Greek. Such is the case in Revelation 7, where we read, for example, in verse 5: Of the tribe of Juda were sealed twelve thousand (chilias, singular). Of the tribe of Reuben were sealed twelve thousand (chilias). Of the tribe of Gad were sealed twelve thousand (chilias). In this case, the word "thousand" is the noun, rather than the adjective. Thus, it does not need to agree with another word grammatically, even though we understand it to be referring to a plural number of Israelites. The word is a collective noun, much as our English words "sheep" or "deer". Thus, it is written in the singular, even though technically there are TWELVE of these "thousands." And so, while we encourage people to use a good concordance, we must yet use some caution and realize our limitations. Therefore, when John tells us in Revelation 20 that some will reign with Christ for a thousand years, the translation is correct, even though chilioi is technically plural. Also we must understand the John is seeing a vision in heaven not on earth. The souls that were beheaded were reigning with Christ for this long period of time, past tense. So according to the Greek grammar there is no such thing as a one thousand year anything. You will not find the numerical "one" any where in that chapter.

THE EARLY CHURCH

Eusebius is one of the early church fathers who most clearly denounce "chiliasm," as premillennialism was then called. In the same work he writes, "About the same time ... appeared Cerinthus, the leader of another Heresy. Caius, in *The Disputation* attributed to him, writes respecting him: 'But Cerinthus, by means of revelations which he pretended as if they were showed him by angels, asserting, that after the resurrection there would be an earthly kingdom of Christ, and that flesh, i.e. men, again inhabiting Jerusalem, would be subject to desires and pleasures. Being also an enemy to the divine scriptures, with a view to deceive men, he said that there would be a space of a thousand years for celebrating nuptial festivals.' Eusebius also writes of a tradition passed down by Polycarp regarding an encounter between the Apostle John and Cerinthus in a public bath, "He [Polycarp] says that John the Apostle once entered a bath to wash; but ascertaining that Cerinthus was within, he leaped out of the place and fled from the door, not enduring to enter under the same roof with him, and exhorting those with him to do the same, saying, 'Let us flee, lest the bath fall in, as long as Cerinthus, that enemy of the truth is within.'"[5] Tertullianus is another early church father who attributes chiliasm's birth to Cerinthus. He writes: "They are not to be heard who assure themselves that there is to be an earthly reign of a thousand years, who think with the heretic Cerinthus. "For the Kingdom of Christ is now eternal in the saints, although the glory of the saints shall be manifested after the resurrection." From Eusebius' *Eccleslastical History*, Book 3, Chapter 23. Circa A.D. 324.

The earliest surviving account of Cerinthus is that in Irenæus' refutation of Gnosticism, *Adversus haereses* (I: xxvi; III: iii and xi), which was written about 170 CE. According to Irenæus, Cerinthus, a man educated in the wisdom of the Egyptians, claimed angelic inspiration. He taught that the visible world and heavens were not made by the supreme being, but by a lesser power (Demiurge) distinct from him. Not Jehovah but the angels have both made the world and given the law. These creator-angels were ignorant of the existence of the Supreme God. The Jewish law remained sacred and essential to salvation.

 Cerinthus distinguished between the man Jesus and the Christ. He denied the supernatural birth of Jesus, making him the son of Joseph and Mary, and distinguishing him from Christ, who descended upon him at baptism and left him again at his crucifixion. Cerinthus is also said to have taught that Jesus will be raised from the dead at the Last Day, when all men will rise with Him.
 He was thus similar to an Ebionite in his Christology, but Gnostic in his doctrine of the creation.
Cerinthus believed in a happy millennium which would be realized

here on earth previous to the resurrection and the spiritual kingdom of God in heaven.

According to Irenaeus, Polycarp told the story that St. John the Divine, in particular, is said to have so feared Cerinthus that he once fled a bathhouse when he found out Cerinthus was inside, yelling "Let us flee, lest the building fall down; for Cerinthus, the enemy of the truth, is inside!"

Among the teachings of Cerinthus that were in opposition to the apostles and other early church fathers:

- A lesser deity created the physical world
- Jesus the man and "Christ" the godly spirit were not one in the same
- Justification by works, in particular the ceremonial observances of Judaism.

Cerinthus may be the alleged recipient of the Apocryphon of James (codex I, text 2 of the Nag Hammadi library), although the name written is largely illegible.

John Calvin (1536)

"But a little later there followed the chiliasts, who limited the reign of Christ to a thousand years. Now their fiction is too childish either to need or to be worth a refutation. And the Apocalypse, from which they undoubtedly drew a pretext for their error does not support them. For the number "one thousand" (Rev. 20:4) does not apply to the eternal blessedness of the church but only to the various

disturbances that awaited the church, while still toiling on earth."
"For when we apply to it the measure of our own understanding, what can we conceive that is not gross and earthly? So it happens that like beasts our senses attract us to what appeals to our flesh, and we grasp at what is at hand. So we see that the Chialists (i.e. those who believed that Christ would reign on earth for a thousand years) fell into a like error. Jesus intended to banish from the disciples' minds a false impression regarding the earthly kingdom: for that, as He points out in a few words, consists of the preaching of the Gospel. They have no cause therefore to dream of wealth, luxury, power in the world or any other earthly thing when they hear that Christ is reigning when He subdues the world to Himself by the preaching of the Gospel. It follows from this that His reign is spiritual and not after the pattern of this world." - Comm. on Acts 1:8 (Torrance, VI, 32).

Philip Schaff (1877)

"Though millennialism was suppressed by the early church, it was nevertheless from time to time revived by heretical sects." (Schaff's History, pg. 299)

Christianity Today

"In *City of God*, Augustine (354-430) viewed the thousand years of Revelation 20 not as some special future time but "the period beginning with Christ's first coming," that is, the age of the Christian church. Throughout this age, the saints reign with Christ—not in the fullness of the coming kingdom prepared for those blessed by God the Father, but "in some other and far inferior way." This position, often called "amillennial," became the view of most Christians in the West, including the Reformers, for almost 1,500 years."

"The days will come in which vines shall grow," imagined Papias of Hierapolis, "each having ten thousand branches, and in each branch ten thousand twigs, and in each true twig ten thousand shoots, and in each one of the shoots ten thousand clusters, and on every one of the clusters ten thousand grapes, and every grape when pressed will give two hundred gallons of wine. And when any of the saints shall lay hold of a cluster, another shall cry out, 'I am a better cluster, take me; bless the Lord through me.'" Papias (c.60-120) was perhaps the first post-biblical author to describe the thousand-year visible Kingdom of Christ—the Millennium." (The End: A History of the Second Coming)

Robert G. Clouse

"the Council of Ephesus in 431, belief in the millennium was condemned as superstitious." (Clouse, *The Meaning of the Millennium*, p. 9.)

James M. Efird (1989)

"If one examines the texts carefully, however, it becomes rather obvious that John is not talking about the earth but is describing a scene in *heaven*. The martyrs are in heaven here and in every other place in Revelation (cf. 6:9-10). These martyrs are reigning with Christ in heaven, not for one thousand literal years but *completely, totally."* (*Revelation for Today: An Apocalyptic Approach,* Nashville, TN: Abingdon Press, 1989, p. 115)

For a thousand years (*chilia ete*). Accusative of extent of time. Here we confront the same problem found in the 1260 days. In this book of symbols how long is a thousand years? All sorts of theories are proposed, none of which fully satisfy one. Perhaps Peter has given us the only solution open to us in 2Pe_3:8 when he argues that "one day with the Lord is as a thousand years and a thousand years as one day." It will help us all to remember that God's clock does not run by ours and that times and seasons and programs are with him. This wonderful book was written to comfort the saints in a time of great trial, not to create strife among them. (**A.T. Robertson Word Picture in the New Testament**)

As we have read there is no such doctrine or teaching within the N.T. or the early church concerning a millennium on earth with a kingdom being established by Jesus. Jesus will return literally and will bring about the resurrection of the dead with judgment for those who did not put their trust or faith in him. We must be ready and living as if Jesus is going to return any day.

BE READY

In conclusion, we need to be ready everyday and continually be living for God as if Jesus is returning at any moment. We can not divide the body of believers over non essentials issues. These issues of how the last days will play out are non essential issues and as long as we agree that Jesus is returning literally then we should not divide the church over this. Paul tells Timothy to look for the blessed hope and the appearing of the glory of our great Elohim and Savior, Messiah Jesus. This should be our goal and our way of living everyday, looking for the return of Jesus and the resurrection of the dead in which we will all be changed into our glorious bodies that has been prepared for us by God.

The message of the gospel is simple; Jesus died, was buried and rose again. The stories people tell about the last days and the end times are just stories. Most of them claim that God showed them what is going to happen or that God gave them special understanding of scripture. Is God the author of confusion? How can these men all be right when they don't agree with each other? Yet they claim God showed them. We must preach the gospel and teach the world that Jesus is real and is returning to judge the world through him. This is the message that we must preach and teach and not get caught up with all this nonsense of who the antichrist is going to be or what role the U.S. is going to play the last days or end times. We need to focus on the lost and preach the death, burial and resurrection of Jesus. Yes he is returning but nobody know when or how for that matter. He could return today, tomorrow or 100 years from now. The point is, he is returning, literally. If you enjoyed this book and it has helped you in understanding the Bible better please visit our website at **www.JudeoChristianInstituteofApologetics.org** and leave us a message.

BIBLIOGRAPHY

Augustine is cited in Henry Alford, *The Greek New Testament*, 4 vols., (Chicago: Moody, rep. 1958 [n.d.]), 2:82. Marvin R. Vincent,

Word Studies in the New Testament (Grand Rapids: Eerdmans, rep. 1946 [1887]), 4:67. A. T. Robertson, *Word Pictures in the New Testament* 4:51. Leon Morris, *The First and Second Epistles to the Thessalonians* (*NICNT*) (Grand Rapids: Eerdmans, 1959), 213.

F. F. Bruce, *New Testament History* (Garden City, N.Y.: Anchor, 1969), 309.

E. Schuyler English, *Rethinking the Rapture* (Neptune, N.J.: Loizeaux, 1954), 72.

Thomas L. Constable, "2 Thessalonians," in John F. Walvoord and Roy B. Zuck, eds., *Bible Knowledge Commentary: New Testament* (Wheaton, Ill.: Victor, 1983), 717.

John F. Walvoord, *Prophecy Knowledge Handbook* (Wheaton, Ill.: Victor, 1990), 493. Lewis Sperry Chafer, *Systematic Theology*, 7 vols., (Dallas: Dallas Seminary, 1948), 6:85.

Charles C. Ryrie, *The Basis of the Premillennial Faith* (Neptune, NJ: Loizeaux, 1953), 151. See also: Charles Lee Feinberg in Feinberg, ed., Prophecy and the Seventies (Chicago: Moody, 1971), 181.

Anthony A. Hoekema, *The Bible and the Future* (Grand Rapids: Eerdmans, 1979), 178.

Donald Guthrie, *New Testament Introduction* (3rd ed.: Downer's Grove, Ill.: InterVarsity Press, 1970), 457-465.

William Hendriksen, *I and II Thessalonians* (NTC) (Grand Rapids: Baker, 1955), 15. Guthrie, *New Testament Introduction*, 566-567, 579. John A. T. Robinson, *Redating the New Testament* (Philadelphia: Westminster, 1976), 53.

F. F. Bruce, *The Book of the Acts* (*NICNT*) (Grand Rapids: Eerdmans, rep. 1980 [n.d.]), 364.

Suetonius, *Claudius* 25:4. Cp. Dio Cassius, *History* 60:6; Orosius, *History*, 7:6:15ff.

Michael Grant, ed., Suetonius, *The Twelve Caesars*, trans. by Robert Graves (London: Penguin, 1979), 202. Bruce, *New Testament History*, 297-299.

The Greek term *antitassomenon* ("opposed") in Acts 18:8 is a military term and indicates organized resistance.

Cf. Matt. 12:43-45; John 8:44; Rev. 2:9; 3:9. In 2 Corinthians Paul mentions Satanic blinding to the gospel (4:4) in the context of making reference to the veil blinding the Jews regarding the New Covenant (3:15; cp. Heb. 8:8-13). He then discusses his own grievous persecution (4:7-18). See my *Before Jerusalem Fell: Dating the Book of Revelation* (Tyler, Tex.: Institute for Christian Economics, 1989), ch. 13.

Page attempts to draw the parallel with Revelation 20, comparing the restraint and deception of Satan and the flaming coming of Christ with the deception, restraint, and coming here. Sydney H. T. Page, "Revelation 20 and Pauline Eschatology," *Journal of the Evangelical Theological Society* 23:1 (March, 1980) 31-44.

There are various Days of the Lord in Scripture. For example, upon Babylon (Isa. 13:9, cp. v.1) and Egypt (Jer. 46:10, cp. vv. 2, 11-14; Eze. 30:36).

See: J. Marcellus Kik, *An Eschatology of Victory* (Nutley, N.J.: Presbyterian and Reformed, 1971), 144-150. David Chilton, *The Great Tribulation* (Tyler, Tex.: Institute for Christian Economics, 1987), 25-28.

Acts 1:4; 1:8; 18:21; 20:16; 24:11. Even in this early post-commission Christianity, believers continued to gravitate toward the Jews: engaging in Jewish worship observances (Acts 2:1ff.; 21:26; 24:11), focusing on and radiating their ministry from Jerusalem (Acts 2-5), frequenting the Temple (Acts 2:46; 3:1ff.; 4:1; 5:21ff.;

21:26; 26:21) and attending the synagogues (13:5, 14; 14:1; 15:21; 17:1ff.; 18:4, 7, 19, 26; 19:8; 22:19; 24:12; 26:11).

For a study of the contra-Jewish function of tongues, which are so detailed in 1 Corinthians, see: Kenneth L. Gentry, Jr., *Crucial Issues Regarding Tongues* (Mauldin, S.C.: GoodBirth, 1982).

David Chilton, *Productive Christians in an Age of Guilt Manipulators* (Tyler, Tex.: Institute for Christian Economics, 1981), 168-170.

Greek: enesteken. A. M. G. Stephenson, "On the meaning of *enesteken he hemera tou kuriou* in 2 Thessalonians 2:2", *Texte und Untersuchungen zur Geshichte der altchristlichen Literatur* 102 (1968) 442-451. William F. Arndt and F. Wilbur Gingrich, *A Greek-English Lexicon of the New Testament* (4th ed.: Chicago: University of Chicago, 1957), 266. See: Morris, *First and Second Thessalonians*, 215. Note the agreement among the following translations: NASB, NKJV, NEB, TEV, Moffatt's New Translation, Weymouth, Williams, Beck.

Constable, "2 Thessalonians," 718. Non-dispensationalist Marshall comments: "The argument is difficult to follow, partly because of the way in which Paul tackles the theme in a non-chronological manner." I. Howard Marshall, *1 and 2 Thessalonians* (*NBC*) (Grand Rapids: Eerdmans, 1983), 185

For political *apostasia* see the Septuagint at Ezra 4:12, 15, 19; Neh. 2:19; 6:6. For religious *apostasia* see the Septuagint at Josh. 22:22; 2 Chr. 29:19; and 33:19, and in the New Testament Acts 21:21.

Hendriksen, *I and II Thessalonians* (*NTC*), 170. Constable, "2 Thessalonians," 718.

See my *Before Jerusalem Fell*, 293-298. Cf. Benjamin B. Warfield, "The Prophecies of St. Paul" in *Biblical and Theological Studies*, ed. by Samuel G. Craig, (Philadelphia: Presbyterian and Reformed, 1952), 473-475.

E.g., Augustine, *City of God* 20:19; Chrysostom cited in Alford, *Greek Testament*, 2:80. If we are correct in equating him with the Beast, we could add: Victorinus, *Apocalypse* 17:16; Lactantius, *On the Death of the Persecutors* 2; Sulpicius Severus, *Sacred History* 2:28, 29. See my *The Beast of Revelation* (Tyler, Tex.: Institute for Christian Economics, 1989).

The view that the Roman government was the restrainer is called by Schaff "the patristic interpretation." Philip Schaff, *History of the Christian Church* (3rd ed: Grand Rapids: Eerdmans, 1910), 1:377n. It was held by Tertullian, *On the Resurrection of the Flesh* 24 and *Apology* 32; Irenaeus, *Against Heresies* 5:25-26; Augustine, *City of God* 20:19; Lactantius, *Divine Institutes*, 7:15.

Trajan, *Epistle* 5; cp. Suetonius, *Nero* 19. See: B. W. Henderson, *The*

Life and Principate of the Emperor Nero (London: Methuen, 1903), ch. 3.

As in Luke 4:29, where the Jews led Jesus to a hill "so as to cast him down" (*hoste katakremnisai auton*). Ernst Best, *Commentary on First and Second Thessalonians* (London: Black, 1977), 286-290. H. E. Dana and Julius R. Mantey, *A Manual Grammar of the Greek New Testament* (Toronto: Macmillan, 1955), 214.

Philo, *Legatio ad Caium* 43, as cited by Eusebius, *Ecclesiastical History* 2:6:2.

The Roman standards were "sacred emblems" (Josephus, Wars 3:6:2). "The camp religion of the Romans is all through a worship of the standards, a setting the standards above all gods" (Apology 16).

W. G. Khmmel, *Introduction to the New Testament,* trans. by Howard Clark Kee (17th ed.: Nashville: Abingdon, 1973), 267. The dispensationalist idea of a rebuilt Temple here has to be read eisegetically into the text, for the reference to the Temple in 2 Thess. 2:4: (1) was written while the Jewish Temple was still standing as the obvious referent, (2) lacks any allusion to a rebuilding of the Temple, and (3) if speaking of a rebuilt Temple, is contrary to the clear, divinely ordained disestablishment of the Temple (e.g., John 4:24; Matt. 24; Hebrews).

Gentry, *Before Jerusalem Fell,* 279-284. Tacitus, *Annals* 15:44.

Such imperial arrogance would produce alleged miracles as confirmation. Vespasian is called "the miracle worker, because by him "many miracles occurred." Tacitus, *Histories* 4:81; Suetonius, *Vespasian* 7. Notice that Paul speaks of these as "lying wonders."

Eusebius, *Ecclesiastical History* 3:5:3; Epiphanius, *Heresies* 29:7. See also: Rev. 7:1-17 in Gentry, *Before Jerusalem Fell*, 243-244.

Daniel's Seventy Weeks

Charles H. H. Wright, *An Introduction to the Old Testament* (London: Williams and Norgate, 1906), p. 197.

John F. Walvoord, *The Rapture Question* (Grand Rapids: Zondervan, 1957), p. 24.

John F. Walvoord, *Daniel: The Key to Prophetic Revelation* (Chicago: Moody, 1971), pp. 201, 216.

Alva J. McClain, *Daniel's Prophecy of the 70 Weeks* (Grand Rapids: Zondervan, 1940), p. 9.

J. Dwight Pentecost, *Things to Come* (Grand Rapids: Zondervan, 1958), p. 240.

E. Schuyler English, "The Gentiles in Revelation," in Charles Lee Feinberg, ed., *Prophecy and the Seventies* (Chicago: Moody, 1971), p. 242.

O. T. Allis, *Prophecy and the Church* (Philadelphia: Presbyterian and Reformed, 1945), p. 111.

J. A. Montgomery, *A Critical and Exegetical Commentary on the Book of Daniel* (*International Critical Commentary*) (New York: Scribner's, 1927), p. 400.

E. J. Young, *The Prophecy of Daniel* (Grand Rapids: Eerdmans, 1949, 1977), p. 191.

E. W. Hengstenberg, *The Christology of the Old Testament* (McLean, VA: McDonald, rep. n.d. [trans. 1854]), 2:803-930.

Robert Duncan Culver, *Daniel and the Latter Days* (2rd ed.: Chicago: Moody, 1977), p. 144. *bid.*, p. 144.

Allis mentions this teaching flowing out of the dispensational approach to Dan. 9:24-27 as "one of the clearest proofs of the novelty of that doctrine as well as of its revolutionary nature." Allis, *Prophecy and the Church*, p. 109. It is in Kline's analysis of Daniel 9 that he is led to call dispensationalism an "evangelical heresy." Meredith Kline, "Covenant of the Seventieth Week," in John H. Skilton, ed., *The Law and the Prophets: Old Testament Studies in Honor of Oswald T. Allis* (n.p.: Presbyterian and Reformed, 1974), p. 452.

Kline, "The Covenant of the Seventieth Week," p. 456.

William Taylor Smith, "Number," in James Orr, ed., *International Standard Bible Encyclopedia* (2nd ed.: Grand Rapids: Eerdmans, 1956), 3:2162.

E. J. Young, "Daniel," in Donald Guthrie and J. Motyer, eds., *Eerdmans Bible Commentary* (Grand Rapids: Eerdmans, 1970), p. 698.

Kline, "Daniel 9," p. 452. Young, *Prophecy of Daniel*, p. 196. C. F. Keil, "Biblical Commentary on the Book of Daniel," in C. F. Keil and Franz Delitzsch, *Commentary on the Old Testament* (Grand Rapids: Eerdmans, rep. 1975), pp. 338-339. Milton S. Terry, *Biblical Apocalyptics: A Study of the Most Notable Revelations of God and of Christ* (Grand Rapids: Baker, rep. 1988 [1898]), p. 201. Montgomery, *Critical and Exegetical Commentary on the Book of Daniel*, pp. 220-221.

Hengstenberg, *Christology of the Old Testament*, 2:880.
Lev. 25:2-5; 26:34, 35, 43; 2 Chron. 36:21; etc.
Hengstenberg, *Christology of the Old Testament*, 2:884ff.

The presence of streets seems to portray a stable, prosperous city open to trade and intercourse; whereas the destruction of streets are foreboding emblems of devastation and judgment. See: 1 Kgs. 20:34; Jer. 7:34; 33:10; 44:6, 17; Zeph. 3:6.

Apparently, Psalm 147:13-14 is praise to the Lord for Nehemiah's rebuilding of Jerusalem. See: J. A. Alexander, *Psalms Translated and Explained* (Grand Rapids: Baker, rep. 1873), p. 557.

J. Barton Payne, *Encyclopedia of Biblical Prophecy* (New York: Harper and Row, 1973), pp. 388ff. C. Boutflower, *In and Around the Book of Daniel* (London: SPCK, 1923), pp. 195ff.

Julius Africanus, in Eusebius, *Demonstration of the Gospel* 8:2. This may be found in Alexander Roberts and James Donaldson, eds., *The*

Ante-Nicene Fathers (Grand Rapids: Eerdmans, rep. 1885), 6:134. For Vitringa and Ideler, see: Hengstenberg, *Christology of the Old Testament*, 2:891 n2. Harold Hoehner, *Chronological Aspects of the Life of Christ* (Grand Rapids: Zondervan, 1977). J. Dwight

Pentecost, "Daniel," in Walvoord and Zuck, *Bible Knowledge Commentary*, pp. 1363-1365.

Ralph Woodrow, *Great Prophecies of the Bible* (Riverside, CA: Woodrow Evangelistic Assoc., 1971, 1989), pp. 94-101. Martin Anstey, *Romance of Bible Chronology* (1913). Ptolemy (A.D. 70-161) has provided us with his important *The Canon of Ptolemy*, upon which much of ancient chronology today is based.

See: Young, "Daniel," in *Eerdmans' Bible Commentary*, p. 699. Hengstenberg, *Christology*, 2:829.

Matt. 11:3; Mark 15:43; Luke 1:76-79; 2:25, 26, 38; 3:15.

See also: Zech. 1:12; 2:1; 7:7; 8:5-6.

Julius Africanus held this view long ago. See his comments cited in Eusebius, *Demonstration of the Gospel* 8:2.

Payne, "Goal of Daniel's Seventy Weeks," p. 111.
This happens with His death, when the veil is rent (Matt. 27:51]).
The definite article, which occurred before "transgression" and "sins," is lacking here. There it referred to the particular situation of Israel. Here it considers the more general predicament of mankind.
Heb. 1:3; 7:27; 9:7-12, 26, 28; 10:9-10. See also: John 1:29; Rom. 3:25; 2 Cor. 5:19; 1 Pet. 2:24; 1 John 2:2.

Walvoord, *Daniel*, pp. 221, 222.

Leon Wood, *A Commentary on Daniel* (Grand Rapids: Zondervan, 1973), p. 250.

Walvoord slips by letting this prophecy cover "the cessation of the New Testament prophetic gift seen both in oral prophecy and in the writing of the Scriptures" (Walvoord, *Daniel*, p. 222). This, however, does not occur in either the first sixty-nine weeks (up to "just before the time of Christ's crucifixion") or in the seventieth week (the future Great Tribulation), the periods which he claims involve the 490 years. John F. Walvoord, *Prophecy Knowledge*

Handbook (Wheaton, IL: Victor, 1990), p. 258. Yet he specifically says that the "six major events characterize the 490 years"! (*Ibid.*, p. 251). After intensive study, I have changed my own view on this passage from an earlier published statement. See Gentry, *The Charismatic Gift of Prophecy: A Reformed Response to Wayne Grudem* (2nd ed: Memphis: Footstool, 1989), p. 54n.

Luke 1:35; cp. 4:34, 41. See also: Mark 1:24; Acts 3:14; 4:27, 30; 1 John 2:20; Rev. 3:7; He is called the "anointed one" (Psa. 2:2; Isa. 42:1; Acts 10:38).

Interestingly there was a current, widely held belief that there was to arise a ruler from in Israel "at that very time," i.e., during the Jewish War. Tacitus, *Histories* 5:13: "The majority were convinced that the ancient scriptures of their priests alluded to *the present as the very time* when the Orient would triumph and from Judaea would go forth men destined to rule the world. This mysterious prophecy really referred to Vespasian and Titus...." Suetonius, *Vespasian* 4: "An ancient superstition was current in the East, that out of Judaea at this time would come the rulers of the world. This prediction, as the event later proved, referred to a Roman Emperor...."Josephus even picks up on this idea, when he ingratiates himself to Vespasian by declaring he was the one to rule (*Wars* 3:8:9). The only prophecy regarding Israel that actually dates Messianic era events is Daniel 9:24-27. Josephus also applies the Daniel 9 passage to the rule of the Romans in another context: "In the very same manner Daniel also wrote concerning the Roman government, and that our country should be made desolate by them. All these things did this man leave in writing, as God had shewed them to him...." (*Ant.* 10:11:7).

Psa. 2:2; 132:10; Isa. 11:2; 42:1; Hab. 3:13; Acts 4:27; 10:38; Heb. 1:9. Vanderwaal denies the Messianic referent of this passage, preferring a Maccabean priestly referent. Cornelius Vanderwaal, *Hal Lindsey and Biblical Prophecy* (St. Catherines, ON: Paideia, 1978), p. 37.

When "covenant" is mentioned in Daniel, it is always of God's covenant, see: Daniel 9:4; 11:22, 28, 30, 32. This includes even Dan. 11:22; see: Pentecost, "Daniel," *Bible Knowledge Commentary*, 1:1369.

His covenants are "the covenants of the promise" (Eph. 2:12). See: Luke 1:72; Acts 3:25-26; 13:32; 26:6-7; Rom. 1:2; 4:16; 9:4; 15:8; 2 Cor. 1:20; Gal. 3:16-22; Eph. 3:6; Heb. 7:22; 13:20.

Matt. 26:28; Mark 14:24; Luke 22:20; 1 Cor. 11:25; 2 Cor. 3:6; Heb. 8:8, 13; 9:15; 12:24.

Deut. 7:9, 21; 10:17; Neh. 1:5; 9:32; Isa. 9:6; Dan. 9:4. Hengstenberg argues convincingly that the source of Daniel 9 seems to be Isaiah 10:21-23, where God is the "Mighty God" who blesses the faithful remnant.

Young, *Daniel*, p. 209; Allis, *Prophecy and the Church*, p. 122;

Hengstenberg, *Christology of the Old Testament*, p. 856.

Its length is alluded to in Luke 13:6-9. His crucifixion after three and one-half years of ministry is widely agreed upon. A. T. Robertson, *A Harmony of the Gospels* (New York: Harper and Row, 1922, 1950), p. 270. Eusebius comments: "since he began his work during the high priesthood of Annas and taught until Caiaphas held the office, the entire time does not comprise quite four years" (*Eccl. Hist.* 1:10:3).

Philip Mauro, *The Seventy Weeks and the Great Tribulation* (Boston: Hamilton, 1923), p. 101. See discussion on his pages 91-101.

Walvoord, *Prophecy Knowledge Handbook*, pp. 256-257. Ryrie, *Basic Theology*, p. 465. Pentecost, "Daniel," *BKC*, 1:161. Walvoord, *Daniel*, pp. 230-231. It is interesting to note that the early Fathers held to a non-eschatological interpretation of the Seventieth Week, applying it either to the ministry of Christ or to A.D. 70. See: Barnabus 16:6; Clement of Alexandria, *Miscellanies* 1:125-26; Tertullian, *An Answer to the Jews* 8; Julius Africanus, *Chronology* 50. See: L. E. Knowles, "The Interpretation of the Seventy Weeks of Daniel in the Early Fathers," *Westminster Theological Journal* 7 (1945) 136-160.

Pentecost, "Daniel," *BKC*, p. 1364. See Walvoord, *The Rapture Question*, p. 25.

Hans K. LaRondelle, *The Israel of God in Prophecy* (Berrien Springs, MI: Andrews University, 1983), p. 173.

Pentecost, "Daniel," *BKC*, p. 1364.

McClain, *Daniel's Prophecy of the Seventy Weeks*, p. 35.

Walvoord, *Daniel*, p. 232.

Walvoord, *Prophecy Knowledge Handbook*, p. 250.

Walvoord, *Daniel*, p. 230.

Ibid., p. 230.

Walvoord, *Rapture Question*, p. 25.

Pentecost, *Things to Come*, p. 198.

Besides this, dispensationalists put asunder what God has joined together. That is, passages such as Isaiah 9:6-7 merge the earthly ministry of Christ with His kingship because they do find fulfillment in, pp. 230-231. *Ibid.*, p. 218.

Robert Anderson, *The Coming Prince* (London: Hodder and Stoughton, 1909). Feinberg, *Millennialism*, p. 150. H. Wayne House and Thomas D. Ice, *Dominion Theology: Blessing or Curse?* (Portland, OR: Multnomah, 1988), p. 321: "Daniel predicted precisely the year in which Messiah would be cut off." Hoehner, *Chronological Aspects of the Life of Christ*, p. 139: "The *terminus ad quem* of the sixty-ninth week was on the day of Christ's triumphal entry on March 30, A.D. 33."

Ryrie, *Basic Theology*, pp. 448, 465.

McClain, *Daniel's Prophecy of the Seventy Weeks*, p. 35.

J. B. Payne, "Goal of Daniel's Seventy Weeks," p. 109.

McClain, *Daniel's Prophecy of the Seventy Weeks*, p. 39.

See the following two chapters for a detailed study of Matthew 24.

Pentecost, "Daniel," *BKC*, p. 1364.

Francis Brown, S. R. Driver, and Charles A. Briggs, eds., *A Hebrew and English Lexicon of the Old Testament* (Rev. ed.: Oxford: Clarendon, 1972), p. 503.

Brown, Driver, Briggs, *Hebrew Lexicon*, p. 149.

Deut. 7:9, 21; 10:17; Neh. 1:5; 9:32; Isa. 9:6; Dan. 9:4. See earlier discussion above.

Kline provides interesting arguments for the reference "the prince who is to come" (v. 27) being to "Messiah the Prince" (v. 25). If this were conclusive, the "he" would then refer back to the Messiah in either view.

Psa. 50:5. Cf.: Exo. 24:8; Lev. 2:13; Num. 18:19; Zech. 9:11. Contra.: Exo. 334:15; 2 Kgs. 17:35; Eze. 44:7.

1
3
6

Made in the USA
Monee, IL
09 March 2023

29498141R00077